THY KINGDOM COME

A Biblical Study of the Kingdom of God

Jim Showers and Chris Katulka
General Editors
The Friends of Israel Gospel Ministry, Inc.

Thy Kingdom Come: A Biblical Study of the Kingdom of God

Copyright © 2019 by The Friends of Israel Gospel Ministry, Inc. Bellmawr, New Jersey 08099

Unless otherwise noted all Scripture quotations are taken from the New King James Version®. Copyright © 1982 by Thomas Nelson, Inc. Used by permission.

All rights reserved. Printed in the United States of America. No part of this book may be reproduced, stored in a retrieval system, or transmitted, in any form or by any means, electronic, mechanical, photocopying, recording, otherwise, without prior written permission of the publisher. For information, address The Friends of Israel Gospel Ministry, Inc. P.O. Box 908 Bellmawr, NJ 08099

ISBN 978-1-930518-00-1

Library of Congress Cataloging-in-Publication Data is on file at the Library of Congress, Washington, DC.

Cover by Catie Almacellas.

Visit our website at foi.org

CONTENTS

	Contributors	5
	Preface	7
1	God's Coming Kingdom: An Introduction *Jim Showers*	9
2	God's Kingdom and Adam *Steve Herzig*	19
3	God's Kingdom Promise to Abraham *Clarence Johnson*	29
4	God's Kingdom and the Mosaic Covenant *Richard Schmidt*	39
5	God's Kingdom and the Davidic Covenant *Tom Simcox*	49
6	God's Kingdom Anticipation in the First Century *Mike Stallard*	57
7	God's Kingdom in the Sermon on the Mount *Chris Katulka*	67
8	God's Kingdom Offered to Israel *Bruce Scott*	77
9	God's Parables of the Kingdom *Clarence Johnson*	87
10	Ministry of the Rejected King *Tom Simcox*	99

11	God's Kingdom in the Olivet Discourse *Steve Herzig*	109
12	God's Kingdom in Acts and the Epistles *Chris Katulka*	117
13	Controversial Teachings on the Kingdom *Mike Stallard*	127
14	God's Millennial Kingdom *Richard Schmidt*	137
15	God's Eternal Kingdom on Earth *Bruce Scott*	147
	Endnotes	155

CONTRIBUTORS

Steve Herzig holds a BA from Kent State University and a BA from Philadelphia College of Bible (now Cairn University.) He is the director of North American Ministries for The Friends of Israel Gospel Ministry, a contributing editor to *Israel My Glory* magazine, and the author of two books on Jewish culture and customs.

Clarence Johnson holds a BS and an MSCC from Philadelphia College of Bible. He is the National Ministries specialist for The Friends of Israel Gospel Ministry, where he headed the former Institute of Jewish Studies after serving as a pastor for more than 30 years.

Chris Katulka holds a BA from Philadelphia Biblical University and a ThM in Old Testament studies from Dallas Theological Seminary. He is the assistant director of North American Ministries for The Friends of Israel Gospel Ministry, the host and Bible teacher for its weekly radio program and podcast, and contributing editor for *Israel My Glory*.

Richard Schmidt holds a DMin from Northland International University. He spent 32 years in the Milwaukee County Sheriff's Office before retiring in 2019. He also served as an associate pastor, has authored several books on Bible prophecy, and is the founder of Prophecy Focus Ministries in Hales Corners, Wisconsin. Richard currently speaks in churches and conferences and leads tours to Israel as a volunteer with The Friends of Israel Gospel Ministry.

Bruce Scott holds a BA from Grace College of the Bible and an MDiv from Central Baptist Theological Seminary. He is the director of Program Ministries for The Friends of Israel Gospel Ministry, a contributor to *Israel My Glory*, and author of the book *The Feasts of Israel: Seasons of the Messiah*.

Jim Showers holds a BA in accounting from Goshen College and both an MDiv and a DMin from Baptist Bible Seminary. He came to The Friends of Israel in 2002 from Baptist Bible College (now Summit

University) and Seminary, where he served as vice president for development. Jim serves as president and executive director of The Friends of Israel Gospel Ministry.

Tom Simcox holds a BS degree from Philadelphia College of Bible and is a Church Ministries representative for The Friends of Israel Gospel Ministry. He taught Bible for many years as adjunct faculty in Philadelphia Biblical University's former Department of Continuing Education, has been a guest lecturer at Word of Life Bible Institute since 1992, and is an award-winning contributing editor to *Israel My Glory*.

Mike Stallard holds a BS from the University of Alabama, MDiv from Liberty Baptist Seminary, and both a master's of sacred theology (STM) in Greek and New Testament literature and PhD in systematic theology from Dallas Theological Seminary. He serves as the director of International Ministries for The Friends of Israel Gospel Ministry after serving as dean of Baptist Bible Seminary and head of its doctoral program. He was a pastor for 31 years and is the founder and current moderator of the Council on Dispensational Hermeneutics.

PREFACE

In the Sermon on the Mount, Jesus taught His disciples the model prayer, what many call the Lord's prayer. Jesus prayed to the Father, "Your kingdom come, Your will be done on earth as it is in heaven" (Mt. 6:10). The Lord's prayer is structured on the hope that one day God's heavenly Kingdom, where He dwells, will prevail on Earth.

For the disciples, the phrase *Thy Kingdom come* would have been cause for shouting, "Amen!" The coming Kingdom was what the Jewish people hoped and prayed for in Jesus' day; it's the foundation of the hope the prophets promised in the Old Testament. In the Gospels, Jesus offered that Kingdom to Israel, but the Jewish leaders rejected His authority to be the One to usher it in.

Immediately prior to His arrest, Jesus' disciples asked what would be the sign of His coming, when He would establish God's Kingdom on Earth. The disciples believed that one day, God would restore His Kingdom; and they were convinced Jesus was the One who would do it. Prior to Jesus' ascension into Heaven, the disciples were still expecting Him to restore the Kingdom to Israel (Acts 1:6–8). But Jesus told them it was not for them to know when God the Father would perform that feat and that they should get busy being His witnesses to the world.

So the burning question is, "Has the restored Kingdom of God come, or is it yet to come?" Furthermore, what will the restored Kingdom look like? Will it be a literal restoration or a spiritual restoration on Earth? How will we know if the Kingdom has been restored on Earth?

Since Jesus ascended to heaven, nothing in history indicates that God's promised Kingdom has arrived. According to the apostle Paul, creation is still waiting for the curse to be lifted—a curse that continues to bring sickness, disease, natural disasters, and death. God's Messiah has not yet taken His rightful seat on the throne of David to rule over the earth with justice and righteousness.

So, either the restored Kingdom is still future; or it is not a literal, physical entity but, rather, a spiritual one. Many in the church today believe the Kingdom of God has come and that the promise to restore the Kingdom is being fulfilled through the church. They see the Kingdom as a spiritual organism, restored on Earth in the hearts of believers. Is this what Jesus meant when He said to pray for the Kingdom to come so that the will of God will be done on Earth as it is in heaven?

This issue is vitally important because a correct biblical understanding of the Kingdom of God and its restoration is critical to understanding what God is doing on Earth. It affects our comprehension of what God has done in the past, what He is doing today, and what He is yet to do. Our view of things to come (eschatology) is formed from our understanding of the restored Kingdom of God.

This book examines the Kingdom of God as it unfolds in Scripture. We believe reading Scripture literally, taking into account its grammatical and historical context, best harmonizes the biblical revelation of God's Kingdom. By unfolding the Kingdom in God's revelation, we see what He teaches us about it; past, present, and future.

This book was created from the theme for the 2019 Friends of Israel National Prophecy Conference. Each chapter was written by one of our speakers. It's not an in-depth theological treatise, although there is a place for such; rather, it is written for the layman to provide a foundation for God's Kingdom, a concept that is so critical for the church today.

From Genesis 1 through Revelation 22, the Kingdom of God guides our understanding of who God is and what His plan is for the ages. He has promised to restore to Earth His Kingdom that was corrupted shortly after the creation. And God tells us His Kingdom will be restored on this earth for an extended time before it is transferred to the new heavens and earth of the eternal state. We will know it has been restored when His will is done on Earth as it is in heaven.

God's purpose in restoring His Kingdom on Earth is to demonstrate to all of His creation that He alone is the One true God of the universe. Jesus testified that God will restore all of creation, so that, as He concluded the model prayer, to God belongs "the kingdom and the power and the glory forever. Amen."

We pray this book brings you a greater understanding of God's Kingdom plan throughout the Scriptures and deepens your faith in the God we love and adore.

Jim Showers and Chris Katulka, Editors

CHAPTER ONE

God's Coming Kingdom: An Introduction

Jim Showers

More than a decade ago, Hollywood popularized J. R. R. Tolkien's classic novel *The Lord of the Rings* by making a movie trilogy. The third segment was titled *The Return of the King*. The title alone conveys an understanding that a long departed king is returning to rule his kingdom. Tolkien's masterpiece is a fictional fantasy filled with many kings and kingdoms that climax with an epic battle when the power of evil is destroyed with the return of the king.

Kingdoms are a common setting for stories. They are a concept the masses easily understand. Kingdoms make a great backdrop, whether they are real or imagined, for books, plays, movies, television shows, miniseries, and historical documentaries. Everyone comprehends that a kingdom is a system of governance led by a sovereign king or queen who rules over a territory, and the subjects who live in the realm are under his or her absolute authority.

Much of human history has been defined by kings and kingdoms. They were around when smaller city-states led by kings were the norm to later times when those small kingdoms were conquered and united into larger nation-states and eventually into many of the modern countries of today.

And yet, as common as kingdoms have been for governing people throughout history, they are not men's inventions. At some point, before creation, in eternity past, the Godhead determined to have a Kingdom, a theocracy, in which God is the sovereign King, ruling over His created realm and subjects. Theocracy literally means "God rules." Within this Kingdom, He would create a specific realm where He would create a being in His image and empower this being to administer this realm of His Kingdom, so His will is done in the realm. It was God's desire that all of His creation would obey and worship Him as the rightful and deserving sovereign of His Kingdom.

KINGDOM CREATED

In Genesis 1 and 2, this description is what we see unfolding during creation. God brought into existence a universe and specific realm, Earth, over which to rule. On Earth He created an environment to foster and support life and then filled it with living beings: birds, fish, and animals. God also brought into existence a being, created in His image, named Adam.

Created from the dust of the earth, Adam could relate to his environment. Brought forth in the image of His Creator, Adam could relate to and communicate with God. Knowing that Adam was in need of a helpmate, God created Eve from Adam. All human beings are descended from one flesh—Adam's.

God endowed Adam with everything necessary to rule over the realm of Earth as His representative. Made in His image, Adam was empowered to administer and have dominion over the realm of Earth as God's representative. God instructed Adam to be fruitful, multiply, fill the realm of Earth, and rule over it.

This is the picture of the Kingdom God desired from before time when He mapped out not only the creation, but all of human history, "declaring the end from the beginning" (Isa. 46:10). It's a Kingdom over which His will and only His will is done. A Kingdom where His creation worships Him. This is the Kingdom of God on Earth.

But shortly after creation, Adam chose to disobey God and eat from the forbidden tree of the knowledge of good and evil. The apostle Paul taught that when Adam sinned, death came on mankind; and we all became sinners (Rom. 5:12, 18). From this point forward in human history, each child would be born with a disposition against God, a sin nature.

It is not man's nature to turn toward God but, rather, to turn away from Him. All men are born God's enemies. Adam's rebellion against God is passed down to all men and women through Adam's seed: "For all have sinned and fall short of the glory of God" (Rom. 3:23). All mankind is polluted with sin. No one chooses to be a sinner, and no one can avoid being one. Our state was determined for us in Adam's act of rebellion against God in the Garden of Eden.

In the moment Adam sinned and joined Satan's rebellion against the Creator, God lost His human representative to rule over the realm of Earth. No longer was anyone qualified to rule over God's Kingdom. Adam delivered the authority of the earthly realm to Satan when he fell. Satan reminded Jesus of this fact when he offered Jesus the authority over the kingdoms of the earth if He would bow down and worship him: "All this authority I will give You, and their glory; for this has been delivered to me, and I give it to whomever I wish" (Lk. 4:6).

Without a representative to rule over and administer the realm of Earth, God's will would no longer be done on Earth as it is in heaven. The impact of Adam's fall befell all God's creation. In judging Adam for his sin, God subjected all creation to the "futility" of man's sin in the "bondage of corruption" as "the whole creation groans and labors with birth pangs together until now" (Rom. 8:20–22). In Genesis 3, God told Adam He was cursing the ground so man, by the sweat of his brow, would toil to grow food; and thorns and thistles would plague him throughout his life.

Woman would now have pain in childbirth because of her part in the rebellion against God. In judging Satan, God gave hope to mankind as He announced a plan to restore His Kingdom on Earth. From the Seed of a woman would come a Son, who would deliver a fatal blow to Satan. However, before He bruised Satan's head, Satan would bruise the Son's heel.

For God to be sovereign over all, He must put down the rebellion of His creation against Him, remove the rebellious ones, reinstate an Adam-like representative to rule over His Kingdom, and restore His Kingdom on Earth. The ultimate judgment for Adam's choice to join Satan's rebellion was death. The final enemy to be destroyed in God's plan is death (1 Cor. 15:26).

KINGDOM RULER

Exactly how God is working out the restoration of His Kingdom on Earth is the unifying theme of the Bible. To accomplish His plan, God must return Earth to the condition it was in before placing the curse of sin on it. From the announcement of a male Child in Genesis 3, it is clear that God will provide another human being to be His representative to take Adam's place and rule over the realm of His Kingdom on Earth.

To qualify for such a unique role, this promised deliverer has to be related to his environment, made out of the dust of the earth like all other human beings, and never have participated in man's rebellion against His Creator. To accomplish God's declaration to bruise Satan's head, this human representative has to be born sinless, apart from the rebellion against God, and remain sinless to defeat Satan. His sinless life also proves He can do the will of His heavenly Father. In other words, He must be like Adam before the fall, human in all regards but without sin.

To bring this promised male Child into the world, God had to provide the appropriate environment in which the Child could be born and raised in the midst of a fallen and rebellious world. To that end, the people to whom the Child of promise would be entrusted had to know God and fear Him. In Genesis 12, God made a covenant with Abraham, promising to bless the entire world through one of his descendants. God planned to raise up a unique nation, later to be called Israel, who would know Him, for the purpose of sending His Seed to bless the world. This Child came to be revealed as the *Mashiach* (Messiah or Christ), the One who is anointed and set apart for God.

But the *Mashiach* must do more than qualify Himself to be Adam's replacement to restore and administer God's Kingdom on Earth. He must also provide a way for man, who joined Satan's rebellion, to be freed from the bondage and penalty of sin. His name, *Yeshua* (Jesus), reveals that He is the Savior who will save mankind from their sin and reconcile mankind to God. Without a way of human restoration, there would not be human subjects in God's restored, earthly Kingdom.

Israel is the conduit through whom God is working His plan to redeem the world and restore His Kingdom. It would take 2,000 years to raise up this nation and prepare it before God sent His Son of promise, the *Mashiach*, to Earth. Over these two millennia, He revealed more of

His plan to restore His Kingdom through the *Mashiach*. God instituted for Israel holidays and a law system designed to teach Israel what He requires to deliver mankind and His creation from the consequences of sin and restore His Kingdom on Earth.

God unfolded the concept of redemption in Scripture. The law of redemption in Leviticus 25 defines the right of a near kinsman to redeem the land of a close relative that was sold for a price. The love story in the book of Ruth revolved around the right of a kinsman, Boaz, to restore Naomi and marry Ruth by redeeming Naomi's land. This is a picture of the work the *Mashiach* would do to buy back the right for man to rule over Earth as God's representative and rescue men from their sin. Those who put their faith in *Yeshua Hamashiach* (Jesus Christ) become the redeemed bride of Christ.

Redemption requires Messiah to pay the redemption price to purchase back man's position to rule over Earth and reestablish the Kingdom of God on Earth. To qualify as a redeemer of men, the Messiah had to be a near kinsman, a blood relative, of Adam. He had to be born of human flesh through a descendant of Adam. Mary's genealogy in Luke 3 traced His descent back to Adam, the son of God.

In the Passover, redemption is defined in terms of an unblemished blood sacrifice. For the saving of man's soul, the shedding of innocent human blood is the price of redemption. God taught in Leviticus 17:11 that the life is in the blood and it is the blood that atones for the soul. Only a blood sacrifice could cover over man's sin. But animals were not sufficient because they were not related to man. A better sacrifice was required to permanently cover man's sin, one who is related by blood to man.

To be born without sin, the Messiah could not be conceived as all other men, with a sin nature. His conception would have to be of God, through the Holy Spirit. Before He could die and pay the redemptive price with His shed blood on the cross, Messiah had to demonstrate He was sinless, tempted in all points like we are but without sin (Heb. 4:15).

To be Adam's replacement to rule and administer God's Kingdom on Earth, He had to be willing to submit to and do the will of His heavenly Father. He also had to perform signs, wonders, and miracles to demonstrate He had the power and authority to reverse the consequences of sin and control the earth for man's good. All of this Christ accomplished during His First Advent on Earth.

And then Christ went to the cross and bore our sins in His body (1 Pet. 2:24), thereby becoming the unblemished, sacrificial Lamb of God who takes away the sin of the world. Rising on the third day, He conquered death and became the firstfruits of the resurrection to everlasting life.

Jesus Christ became the fulfillment of God's promise to send a male Child to restore His Kingdom. He is the realization of the covenant promise God made to Abraham to bless the world through his Seed. Paul confirmed in Galatians 3:16 that Christ is the fulfillment of the Seed-promise God made to Abraham in Genesis 12:3. It is not a coincidence that Paul referred to Jesus as the last Adam in 1 Corinthians 15:45. By using this title for Christ, he identified Him as the only other person in all of human history who is qualified to rule over the Earth to administer God's Kingdom. The title *last Adam* also indicates that once He comes to rule, He will be God's last human representative to rule over Earth.

KINGDOM RESTORED

During His First Advent, on a day when Jesus was praying, His disciples asked Him to teach them how to pray. His model prayer, recorded in Matthew 6 and Luke 11, is familiar to Christians. He begins by acknowledging our heavenly Father and praising His name. Then Jesus instructed us to petition God, "Your Kingdom come. Your will be done on earth as it is in heaven." First on Jesus' prayer list is the return of God's Kingdom on Earth.

The restoration of God's Kingdom was a priority for Christ, and it should be for us as well. In instructing us how to pray, Jesus disclosed the reason why the coming Kingdom is so important: so God's will is done here on Earth as it is done in heaven. In heaven, His creation continually obeys God's will, the way it was on Earth before the fall. It implies there is a time coming when God's Kingdom will be restored on Earth to the way it was before the fall of man.

Think about it. There has not been one day since Adam's fall that God's will has been done on Earth by all of His creation as it is in heaven. We live with the expectant hope that the world will not continue in sin. Evil will not prevail. God will clean up man's mess and right the consequences of sin through His Son, the Messiah. Jesus would not have told us to pray for God's coming Kingdom if it were not certain to happen.

Jesus concluded the model prayer as He began—with a praise of God, "For Yours is the kingdom and the power and the glory forever." In this short prayer, we see the emphasis on God's Kingdom. To God belong the Kingdom, power, and glory for all eternity. The restoration of God's Kingdom on Earth is a priority of history.

Jesus' model prayer presumes His followers are familiar with the Kingdom of God. He spends no time defining or explaining it. His focus is on the desire for the Kingdom to come, at which time Earth looks much like heaven in regard to God's will. Through the prophets, Israel lived in anticipation of the coming Kingdom of God. The restored Kingdom offered them an end to the oppression and injustice they experienced daily. Isaiah foretold that Earth's government will be on Messiah's shoulders and the rule and peace He brings to Earth will never end. His government will be established with judgment and justice from that time forward and forever (Isa. 9:6–7). During this time, God promised to make Israel the favored nation of the world who leads the other nations in worship of Messiah.

During His earthly ministry, Jesus told the Jewish people that the Kingdom of God was at hand. Jesus the Messiah, the One who could usher in the restored Kingdom of God, was in their midst. Yet He failed to restore God's Kingdom on Earth during His First Advent. Why? Because He was never accepted as their Messiah. He left Earth with the promise to return the next time as the conquering King of kings and Lord of lords.

Peter taught in Acts 3, that Christ will not return to Earth until the Jewish people repent of their sins and accept Jesus as their Messiah. The repentance of the Jewish people, described in Zechariah 12, is yet to happen. Paul said that someday "all Israel will be saved" (Rom. 11:26). Until that day, when the times of refreshing and the restoration of all things come, Peter said Jesus Christ is in heaven waiting for the time of His return.

As in the day Jesus taught His disciples how to pray, His expectation today is that His followers understand the Kingdom of God and its importance. Within the church there is general acceptance for the concept of God's Kingdom but tremendous diversity in the understanding of the form and timing of the coming, restored Kingdom.

Many Christians today believe the Kingdom of God on Earth has transitioned from a physical, political Kingdom on Earth in Genesis 1 and 2 to a spiritual, mystical Kingdom alive in the hearts of believers. They believe the restored Kingdom is alive within everyone who professes faith. Consequently, the church is the Kingdom Jesus commanded us to pray would come.

There is uncertainty by those who hold this view whether the church is God's agent that will someday bring all people to faith in Christ, opening the way for His return, or whether the church simply is a counter to the evil in the world and will continue until Christ's return. This view also sees no rationale for a literal, restored Kingdom of God on Earth. They believe that at His return, Christ will judge the rebellious ones and then take all true believers to the eternal state of Revelation 21 and 22. After two millennia of church history, what is evident today is that evil continues to prevail on Earth and the world seems no closer to the refreshing God promised.

Certainly, the Bible teaches that those who profess faith in Christ become citizens of the Kingdom of God. But being a citizen of the Kingdom doesn't automatically mean the restored Kingdom has come. It simply means our position within the future, physically restored Kingdom of God is secured in Christ. It does not mean, nor does the Bible teach, that the body of believers in the church has become the restored Kingdom in a spiritual form on Earth. Nor does it teach that the church is God's agent to repair the world. Jesus earned that right by shedding His blood, and only He is qualified to restore God's Kingdom. To ascribe it to the church denies Christ the glory due Him.

Scripture speaks of a literal, political, restored Kingdom of God on Earth. For God to fail to install it and leave Earth in its sin-cursed condition would mean He was not able to overcome the bondage of corruption and undo the consequences of the creation's rebellion against its Creator. The restoration and redemption language of God's Word speaks of a literal return of Earth to its condition before the fall when God's representative, the Lord Jesus Christ, will sit on David's throne in Jerusalem and complete man's rule over Earth that Adam lost.

It isn't until the end of His thousand-year reign, when Christ has defeated the final rebellion of Satan, put all of God's enemies under His feet, and destroyed the last enemy of death, that Christ will deliver His Kingdom rule back to God, so "God may be all in all" (1 Cor. 15:24–28). Only then will God take the righteous to live with Him and Jesus Christ in the eternal state.

This study of God's Kingdom to come will examine the unfolding concept of the Kingdom and its restoration on Earth through the progress of God's revelation. It will make the case for a literal, restored Kingdom on Earth, not just a spiritually restored Kingdom through the church because this is what God teaches in His Word. If you are a believer in Jesus Christ, this is your blessed hope and glorious future; so get ready for what God has in store for you.

CHAPTER TWO

God's Kingdom and Adam

Steve Herzig

Get two Jewish people together, and you get three opinions. This saying is a humorous way to say that Jewish people, of which I am one, are opinionated, independent thinkers. For those who know Jewish people, it is no surprise that we have perfected the art of disagreement. However, one area Jewish people are in almost total agreement is Jewish prayer.

That's right, Jewish prayer. The reason is simple: Almost all Jewish prayers begin with these words: *Baruch atah Adonai Eloheinu, melech ha'olam*, "Praised be Thou, O Lord our God, King of the universe." Most Jews are taught to memorize this phrase. All sects of Judaism (Orthodox, Conservative, and Reform) use it in their prayers.

Contained in this prayer is an acknowledgement of God as the King of the universe. Such acknowledgement, if truly believed, is an important step to a better understanding of who the King is. Note that Bible-believing Christians strongly agree that God is the King of the universe.

How is it that a Christian can say "Amen" to a Jewish prayer to the God of the universe? The answer is found in the Jewish Scriptures. First Chronicles 29:11–12 put it this way: "Yours is the kingdom, O Lord, and You are exalted as head over all. Both riches and honor come from You, and You reign over all." The psalmist simply said, "His kingdom rules over all" (Ps. 103:19).

New Testament writings concur. The apostle Paul wrote, "Now to the King eternal, immortal, invisible, to God who alone is wise, be honor and glory forever and ever. Amen" (1 Tim. 1:17). Bible scholar Alva

J. McClain wrote, "Because in His Universal Kingdom God controls the processes of material nature, He is able by such means to control the circumstances of human existence and thereby direct the stream of history."[1] As the King of the universe, He is the reason for all things seen and unseen.

In Genesis 1—3, we see the King of the universe in action as Creator, Commander, King of the corrupted Kingdom, and the coming Messiah. These chapters are foundational to understand the King, His Kingdom, and His relationship with Adam and mankind today.

THE KING AS CREATOR (GENESIS 1:1—2:4)

Genesis 1:1 begins with these words: *Bere'shiyt bara Elohim*, "In the beginning God." These foundational words define the rest of the biblical narrative. Believe them, and you can believe the rest. Reject them, and you are a fool (Ps. 14:1); and the rest of Scripture is utter foolishness to you. These first words, written by Moses, assume God is the uncaused cause as he elaborated in Psalm 90:2: "Before the mountains were brought forth, or ever You had formed the earth and the world, even from everlasting to everlasting, You are God." The Creator of the universe asked Job, "Where were you when I laid the foundations of the earth? Tell Me, if you have understanding. Who determined its measurements? Surely you know! Or who stretched the line upon it?" (Job 38:4–5).

As the Creator, God is self-existent and all powerful, "from everlasting to everlasting." He told Moses, "I AM WHO I AM" (Ex. 3:14). The prophet Isaiah put it this way: "For thus says the LORD, who created the heavens, who is God, who formed the earth and made it, who has established it, who did not create it in vain, who formed it to be inhabited: 'I am the LORD, and there is no other'" (Isa. 45:18). To be sure, anyone who acknowledges the King of the universe—God—as self-existing is taking a leap of faith. Yet believing that, instead of God, matter always existed and formed the universe involves a much bigger leap.

Genesis 1:1 continues with "created the heavens and the earth." *Bara*, the Hebrew word for "created," is used only with God as the subject, never man. God alone created it all. He took nothing and made something—the universe and everything in it—out of it.

His method for creation was speaking. He spoke the universe into existence. Six times in Genesis 1 (vv. 3, 6, 9, 11, 14, 20) the Bible says, "God said, 'Let there be'" or let something come into being; and there was. When He finished creating, the text says, "God saw." Thus, the King made it all, saw it all, and after He finished it all, pronounced it all "very good" (v. 31).

The Hebrew word translated "God" in verse 1 is *Elohim*, the plural form of *El*. That's important because it provides a clue to a deeper understanding of the Creator. Most Hebrew scholars explain it away, saying that *Elohim* is used to denote plural majesty or the "royal we," which presents God's majesty or royalty. But Genesis 1:26 says, "Let Us make man in Our image, according to Our likeness." While the claim for a triune God cannot be made here, the text does suggest a plurality.[2]

A natural question arises from reading Genesis 1. How long is a day? Some of the greatest theological and scientific minds have produced untold volumes of books, articles, and videos to answer that question. An ordinary reading of the text says simply "the evening and the morning" after each day of creation (vv. 5, 8, 13, 19, 23, 31). Thus, we can assume each day was twenty-four hours long.

Furthermore, creation is summed up like this: "The heavens and the earth, and all the host of them, were finished. And on the seventh day God ended His work which He had done, and He rested on the seventh day from all His work which He had done" (2:1–2). Moses reaffirmed the six days of creation in Exodus 20:11: "For in six days the LORD made the heavens and the earth, the sea, and all that is in them and rested the seventh day." God finished His work in six days and rested on the seventh, not because He was tired but because this action teaches us to follow the same principle.

Another question arises from this passage: What was created? Each day's creation tells us a little about the Creator's attributes.

Day 1, "Let there be light" (Gen. 1:3–5). Before the sun was made, God brought forth light. This biblical fact pictures the King as light in its purest form. There is no darkness in Him. He is separate and holy.

Day 2, "Let there be a firmament" (vv. 6–8). A firmament is an expanse or atmosphere, dividing sky from heavens. The King exerted His power by separating and maintaining the atmosphere. As the sky and the heavens are vast, so is the King.

Day 3, "Let there be...dry land" (vv. 9–13). God separated the water to reveal dry ground. Once the ground appeared, grass, vegetation, fruit trees, and their seeds appeared. Here the King demonstrated His authority over creation by separating the heaven and sky, oceans and continents, allowing the earth to raise up vegetation for food for future created beings.

Day 4, "Let there be lights...to divide the day from the night" (vv. 14–19). By creating the sun, moon, and stars, the King demonstrated He is faithful. The cycle of light and darkness is ongoing.

Day 5, "Let the waters abound with an abundance of living creatures" (vv. 20–23). The King demonstrated He is life-giving.

Day 6, "Let the earth bring forth the living creature according to its kind.... Let Us make man in Our image" (vv. 24–27). The King is love, creating diverse creatures to live and thrive on the earth.

Man was not like any other creature in the Garden of Eden; he was the crown jewel of all the King created. God made Adam "from the dust of the ground" (possibly from a play on the Hebrew word *adamah*, meaning "earth"). The King actually "breathed into his nostrils the breath of life" (2:7). Out of everything He created, He made only man in His image and according to His likeness (1:26). No other creature could make this claim.

Like all men and women after him, Adam possessed a body, soul, and spirit. Like the King, he possessed intellect (he could think cognitively, e.g., he named all the animals, 2:19), emotion (anger, love, joy, compassion, etc.), and will (choice). After God created Adam, He knew he was incomplete, so He took his rib from his side (v. 22) and made a woman, Eve. When Adam met her, he said, "This is now bone of my bones and flesh of my flesh; she shall be called Woman, because she was taken out of Man" (v. 23). Adam and Eve were the first married couple, and we learn that marriage was not made in heaven but in Eden.

THE KING AS COMMANDER (GENESIS 1:28–30; 2:15–17)

As Commander-in-Chief of Eden, the King made all the rules and enforced them. They were not suggestions. These commands were: (1) "Be fruitful and multiply" (1:28); (2) "fill the earth and subdue it" (v. 28); (3) "have dominion over the fish of the sea, over the birds of the air, and over every living thing that moves on the earth" (v. 28); (4) "tend and keep" the Garden of Eden (2:15); (5) "Of every tree of the garden you may freely eat" (v. 16); (6) "of the tree of the knowledge of good and evil you shall not eat," the only negative command (v. 17). Everything Adam and Eve needed to live an abundant, thriving life was in the Garden, and the King provided it all: "The LORD God made every tree grow that is pleasant to the sight and good for food" (2:9). Adam had no weeds to pull, he didn't sweat, and he knew no anxiety in his life. He and Eve walked freely in the Garden and ate from any tree they wanted, except for one. Eden was a wonderful place because there was no sin. So uncorrupted were the man and woman that they were completely unaware they were naked; they had no shame (v. 25). Now, this was Kingdom living!

How long and how much Adam and Eve thought about the one negative command no one knows. What we do know is that as long as they remained loyal to the King's command and did not betray Him, their life in the Garden would be "very good." Breaking the law would bring the death penalty, a consequence that would devastate everything created. To what extent Adam and Eve understood death is unknown. What we do know, based on Eve's conversation with the serpent, is that they knew what the King meant when He said, "you shall not" (3:2–3, 17).

The text goes on to explain that the death penalty would mean the breakup of a unique fellowship Adam and the King enjoyed. It would separate him from the King; kick him out of his home; and force him to live outside the place of protection, provision, and perfection he and Eve enjoyed in Eden. They would lose access to the tree of life. Thus their bodies would age, give out, and die, returning to the dust of the earth (vv. 17–19).

THE KING OF THE CORRUPTED KINGDOM (GENESIS 3:1–14)

William Griffith Thomas, theologian, pastor, and cofounder of Evangelical Theological College (later called Dallas Theological Seminary), said Genesis 3 is "the pivot of the Bible." This is the chapter that explains actions like jealousy, cheating, murder, and wickedness. In other words, this is the chapter that explains the world we live in today. From that day on, people have done things their own way and will continue to do so until God restores mankind and establishes His eternal Kingdom. By eating the forbidden fruit, Eve and Adam acted independently and did things their way, not the King's way.

"There is a way that seems right to a man, but its end is the way of death" (Prov. 14:12). Adam and Eve's disobedience proved they wanted to be in charge of the Kingdom and make their own law. This action was cataclysmic and changed everything in creation. Adam and Eve seemed to realize this situation immediately, as they tried to hide from the omniscient God from whom nothing is hidden (Ps. 147:5; Heb. 4:13), claiming to be ashamed of their nakedness (Gen. 3:8–10). Of course, God knew where they were.

The situation described is a commentary on the change that occurred in Adam's heart and the shame he experienced because of his action. Adam and Eve knew what they had done and, as a result, for the first time hid from their King.

"Who told you that you were naked?" God asked them (v. 11). How could Eve and Adam, created "good" and without sin, disobey their King? Genesis 3:1 provides the answer by introducing the tempter: "The serpent was more cunning than any beast of the field." The serpent was an instrument of Satan (Rom. 16:20; Rev 12:9; 20:2). Interestingly, he is the only one in the Kingdom, other than man, who had the ability to speak.

He spoke in half-truths, which really are whole lies, planting doubts in Eve's mind: "Has God indeed said, 'You shall not eat of every tree of the garden'? You will not surely die. For God knows that in the day you eat of it your eyes will be opened, and you will be like God, knowing good and evil" (Gen. 3:1, 4–5).

"What he did not say," theologian John F. Walvoord wrote, "was that they would know the good without being able to do it and know the evil without being able to avoid it."[3] According to radio pastor J. Vernon McGee, "Righteousness is innocence that has been maintained in the presence of temptation."[4] It is not known why Satan approached Eve, rather than Adam. He evidently saw her as an easier target. Adam may have told her what God had told him, which may be why she answered the serpent with semiaccurate information. She even added something God had not said: "nor shall you touch it."

With doubt planted in her mind, Eve "saw that the tree was good for food, that it was pleasant to the eyes, and a tree desirable to make one wise, she took of its fruit and ate. She also gave to her husband with her, and he ate" (v. 6). That temptation became the prescription for other temptations noted in Scripture: "For all that is in the world—the lust of the flesh, the lust of the eyes, and the pride of life—is not of the Father but is of the world" (1 Jn. 2:16). Satan tried tempting Jesus in the wilderness (Mt. 4; Mk. 1; Lk. 4).

Eve, falling to the temptation that appealed to her flesh, eyes, and desires, "took of its fruit and ate" (Gen. 3:6). She then persuaded Adam, who was right by her side, to eat it too. At that moment the Kingdom became corrupted and was in need of redemption.

THE KING AS THE COMING MESSIAH (GENESIS 3:15)

What a mess! The first humans violated the one negative law in the Kingdom. As a result, the King, whose attributes of holiness and righteousness cannot be compromised, had to carry out the sentence. The serpent, who seems to be satanically inspired (Rev. 12:9), questioned the King's rule and planted doubt in Eve's mind, leading her to sin. She then led Adam to sin as well. The consequences were felt in all of creation.

Consequently, the serpent was "cursed more than all cattle" and lost his legs: "On your belly you shall go, and you shall eat dust" (Gen. 3:14).

Eve (and all future women) would have pain in childbirth, and her relationship with her husband (and all future marriages) was under attack: "I will greatly multiply your sorrow and your conception; in pain you shall bring forth children; your desire shall be for your husband, and he shall rule over you" (v. 16).

Adam's work became difficult, and he would eventually die: "In the sweat of your face you shall eat bread till you return to the ground, for out of it you were taken; for dust you are, and to dust you shall return" (v. 19).

Furthermore, both Adam and Eve had to leave the Garden: "The LORD God sent him out of the garden of Eden" (v. 23).

Adam and Eve's disobedience corrupted the whole world. They were left helpless and hopeless, discouraged and depressed. Hiding from the King seemed like their only option since they knew they deserved judgment. It is said that the darker the night, the more glorious the sunrise. This was a dark night for all of the King's creation.

Yet, there was hope: "I will put enmity between you and the woman, and between your seed and her Seed; He shall bruise your head, and you shall bruise His heel" (3:15). Here is the light in the darkness, the good news. The reason: a serpent-Slayer is promised. He is called the "Seed of the woman" (therefore, not of man) who will come to defeat the serpent. Bible scholar and Jewish believer Arnold Fruchtenbaum wrote of this verse: "It is no surprise that the very first messianic prophecy should occur within the context of the Fall. If sin had not entered the world, there would never have been a need for a redeeming Messiah."[5] If God were really all-knowing, as the Bible claims (Ps. 147:5; Heb. 4:13), then He would be ready to predict the coming of Christ immediately after the Fall occurred.

Michael Vlach, a theology professor, wrote, "The coming deliverer must rule from the same realm as Adam. This will relate to the coming Last Adam (1 Cor. 15:45) and His successful kingdom reign over the earth."[6]

Two questions arise from this verse of hope in Genesis 3. Who is He who is to come? When does He arrive? It seems Eve thought the child who fulfilled this promise was her firstborn, Cain: "I have acquired a man from the LORD," she said (Gen. 4:1). A more literal translation says, "I have gotten a man: the LORD [YHWH]" or "I have received a man, namely Jehovah." Walter C. Kaiser Jr, a professor of Old Testament, put it this way: "If this suggestion is correct, then Eve understood that the promised male descendant of human descent would be, in some way, divine, 'the LORD.' If so, then Eve's instincts about the coming Messiah were correct, but her timing was way off!"[7]

Rabbi Akiba, a highly respected ancient sage, was required reading for me as a young boy in Hebrew school. He admitted in the *Midrash Rabbah* (Jewish commentary) that the Hebrew construction of Genesis 4:1 implies that Eve thought she was begetting YHWH. "*The Jerusalem Targum*, an Aramaic translation reads: 'I have gotten a man: the angel of Jehovah.' The Rabbis gave a reading here which is much closer to the original Hebrew text. *The Targum Pseudo-Jonathan* reads, 'I have gotten for a man the angel of the Lord.'"[8] The *Targum*s often substituted "Angel of God" for "God."

Eve believed a special male Child was coming to fix the Kingdom she and Adam corrupted. She was right. However, that Child was not coming from her. As the Bible unfolds God's plan for the ages, it provides a more detailed description of this promised serpent-Slayer.

This Redeemer to come would need the ability both to bring mankind to a right relationship with God and, as the serpent-Slayer, to fix the cursed planet as well. In doing so, He would take His place as the second—the last—Adam.

As the biblical narrative continues, the Holy Spirit takes the wide swath of possibilities and slowly but surely narrows them to ultimately identify the King of the universe, the Lord Jesus Christ. Thus, we can pray, "Praised be Thou, O Lord our God, King of the universe."

CHAPTER THREE

God's Kingdom Promise to Abraham

Clarence Johnson

Not knowing what would lie ahead, on July 20, 1969, astronaut Neil Armstrong stepped out of a tiny lunar module onto the dust-covered terrain of the moon. The world watched and waited to hear his reaction. His historic words were, "That's one small step for man, one giant leap for mankind." Those words were a wonderful commentary on that momentous occasion.

Thousands of years earlier, a man known to us as Abraham took an even greater leap for mankind as he stepped out of Haran onto the dusty soil of the Promised Land. To understand that leap, we need to understand God's covenant with Abraham.

The crimson cord of redemption and the golden cord of Kingdom restoration are inseparably entwined throughout the biblical account past, present, and future. The restoration of the disrupted earthly Kingdom cannot occur without a reversal of the consequences of man's sin. And that reversal can only be accomplished through a redemptive intervention. Redemption is the foundation on which the Kingdom's restoration depends.

MAN'S PATH OF REBELLION

All creation groaned under the weight of the catastrophic transformation that stemmed from Adam and Eve's rebellion in the Garden of Eden. With each subsequent generation, the hope of the promised Redeemer and a restored garden faded. The cursed and corrupt populace of Earth morally deteriorated with such intensity that God declared, "The wickedness of man was great in the earth, and that every intent of the thoughts of his heart was only evil continually. And the earth was filled with violence…all flesh had corrupted their way on the earth" (Gen. 6:5, 11–12).

The grieving Creator caused a universal flood on the earth, destroying humans and beasts, except for one family: Noah's. Noah was a just man who walked with God and found grace in the Lord's eyes. He and his family were divinely rescued in a floating ark; and, once the waters receded, it was time for a fresh start on Earth (chaps. 6—8).

In a manner similar to Adam in Genesis 1:28–30, God blessed Noah and his sons. He gave all living things into their hands and directed them to be fruitful and fill the Earth. For five generations, their families proliferated.

The flood did not impede the great rebellion, which began in the Garden and continued to grow in the hearts and lives of the postflood population. God warned Noah of this situation when He said, "The imagination of man's heart is evil from his youth" (8:21).

Instead of turning to God, Noah's multiplying descendants selected an area of land to live in, built a great city, and raised a tower to the heavens. Their goals were to create a kingdom, make a name for themselves, and elude being scattered across the globe. By refusing to disperse and fill the Earth, they stood in arrogant defiance of God's command. So God thwarted their unified rebellion and counterfeit kingdom. He confused the languages of the various family groups, so they would be incapable of understanding one another. Unable to communicate, they scattered, establishing themselves into distinctively organized groups known as nations (chaps. 10—11).

By Genesis 11, it was evident that mankind rested their fate in their human ability to rule their personal lives and establish an earthly kingdom. They wholeheartedly refused to accept the truth that, without divine intervention, a reversal of the consequences of sin did not lie within their ability or nature. They denied that the promised Redeemer of Genesis 3:15 is the only remedy for sin.

GOD'S DESIGN FOR REDEMPTION

But God continued to fulfill His promise. Tracing His plan of redemption and restoration is like mapping out the path of a river as it travels through a variety of terrains on its long and winding journey. From the springs of inception, the flow moves at an ever-changing pace around, through, and over obstacles as it grows in scope and influence. Sometimes hidden and sometimes a visible torrent, the flow maneuvers through narrow channels and across broad plains.

Determined in eternity past, God's path toward Kingdom restoration was initiated through Adam and Eve and, from there, moved through the turbulent and undulating conduit of humanity's expansion and development. The path flows from a single couple into the broad preflood population. The flood, once again, quickly guided the plan along its way through the narrows of Noah and his family. Then, meandering through the widening progeny of Noah and his sons, the conduit for fulfillment came to rest on the line of Shem (9:26–27).

Until Genesis 12, the identity of the bruised Seed of the woman was shrouded in silence. No further information regarding His appearance or prophesied crushing blow to the serpent was revealed since the initial promise was given. Yet God brought the crimson cord of redemption and the golden cord of restoration to the forefront of history's narrative. Subsequently, with pinpoint accuracy, the Lord fused the flow of the promised redemption, reversal, and restoration into one channel. God's redemptive plan now focused on one man, Abram.

Abram was in the tenth generation of the line of Shem. He and his wife, Sarai, who was barren, lived in Ur of the Chaldeans with his father, Terah. The family moved from Ur to Haran in the land of Canaan, which appears to be contrary to God's order of things in Genesis 9:26–27. The curse on Canaan declared that his descendants were to be subservient to Shem's descendants and dwell in their lands under their authority. But Abram's father moved the family to Haran, in the midst of the land of Canaan, until Terah died (11:10–32).

GOD'S COVENANT WITH ABRAHAM

Why would God choose Abram? A search of Scripture reveals nothing to commend him to God at the time of His call. During the precovenant years, Abram's father and evidently the rest of the family worshiped false gods (Josh. 24:2–3). It is also important to note that Abram's initial response to the Almighty's approach was not immediate. Comparing Genesis 11:31—12:2 with Acts 7:2–4, we learn that God's encounter with Abram in Haran was His second call to him. It was preceded by an initial appearance in Ur that Abram apparently disregarded. God's call to Abram is recorded in Genesis 12:1–3. It includes a call to follow the Lord's leading and the offer of numerous promises of blessing and provision:

> *Now the LORD had said to Abram: "Get out of your country, from your family and from your father's house, to a land that I will show you. I will make you a great nation; I will bless you and make your name great; and you shall be a blessing. I will bless those who bless you, and I will curse him who curses you; and in you all the families of the earth shall be blessed."*

These words are the initial declaration of what is commonly known as the Abrahamic Covenant. The impact of the promises grows in magnitude from personal, to national, and then to universal in nature. Simply stated, before there is any response from this pagan man, God committed Himself to Abram to (1) provide a land for him, (2) make him into a great nation, (3) bless him and make his name great, (4) make him a blessing to others, (5) bless those who bless him, (6) curse those who curse him, and (7) bless all the nations in the world through him.

PROMISED BLESSINGS

The promise to bless Abram and make his name great was a personal commitment to the individual. The promise to make him a great nation was made to a man whose name meant "exalted father," yet he had no children. The scope of the promise grows from the one, Abram, to include a nation that would be great. This promise, therefore, referred to a future group of people not in existence at that time, to eventually be known as Israel.

The Hebrew word for nation is gôy. H. C. Leupold explained:

> *The term gôy is used especially to refer to specifically defined political, ethnic or territorial groups of people.... Thus, in Gen 10:5 the writer speaks of defined groups of people according to their territories.... In this general ethnic sense the term may even be used of Abraham's seed. Thus God said to Abraham, "I will make of you a great nation," i.e. a political, territorial, identified people (Gen 12:2; 17:20; 21:18).*[1]

In Genesis 17, when God reconfirmed the promise of a seed, He changed Abram's name to Abraham because he would be the "father of many nations." Finally, God's planned and promised blessings were not limited to Abraham and Israel. They were to be the conduit of universal blessings to all the nations of the world. The statement and promise of blessings moves from the individual, to the nation, to the universal.

UNILATERAL AND UNCONDITIONAL COVENANT

These promises to Abraham were also unilateral and unconditional, immutable and irrevocable, eternal and everlasting, as well as literal. They required nothing of Abraham. They were gifts of God's grace, freely offered, and ready to be received through faith.

James Boice articulately defined this covenant in his Genesis commentary:

> *What is a covenant? It is a promise—in this case, a promise made by God to Abram. For many of us, "promise" is a better word than "covenant," for "covenant" suggests a bargain and God's covenants are established apart from the bargaining capacities of people.*
>
> *What are the characteristics of God's promises? First, they are unilateral; they are established by God alone. Second, they are eternal and irrevocable. Third, they are based on grace; no people or individual deserves the promises that God makes. These three points are seen in the life of Abram.*[2]

The covenant ceremony in Genesis 15 corroborates the nature of God's promises to Abraham. Verse 18 tells us that the Lord literally "cut a covenant." The phrase may simply imply making a covenant with someone. However, it is commonly believed that ancient ceremonies to seal covenant agreements involved the sacrifice of animals. As H. C. Leupold explained, "The expression *karath berith*, 'to cut a covenant,' results from the butchering of the victims that were slain in the ceremonies attendant upon the conclusion of a covenant."[3]

When the negotiations were finalized, the contractual parties walked a path between the severed bodies of animals that had been cut in two and laid opposite one another. Such an act declared an agreement that the same fate should also fall on any party that ceased to honor his contract. While historical evidence of the practice is minimal, God used this same ceremonial image in Jeremiah 34:18 in reference to His relationship with Israel.

The fulfillment of these promises is unilateral and unconditional, resting solely on God's provision. God—and God alone—symbolically represented as a smoking oven and burning torch, passed through the severed animals while Abraham slept (Gen. 15:17-18).

Leupold continued his explanation:

It should not be forgotten that the covenants God makes with men are not mutual agreements as between man and man. They are rather agreements emanating from God. For in the nature of the case here are not two parties who stand on an equal footing. In fact, in the instance under consideration God binds Himself to the fulfillment of certain obligations; Abram is bound to no obligations whatsoever.[4]

Regarding the unconditional, everlasting, irrevocable, and literal nature of the Abrahamic Covenant, John F. Walvoord presented ten reasons for the unconditional nature of this covenant. In reason four, he stated:

The Abrahamic Covenant was solemnized by a divinely ordered ritual symbolizing the shedding of blood and passing between the parts of the sacrifice... This ceremony was given to Abraham as an assurance that his seed would inherit the land in the exact boundaries given to him in Genesis 15:18–21. No conditions whatever are attached to this promise in this context.[5]

IMMUTABLE AND IRREVOCABLE COVENANT

God cannot lie. His plans, including His Word and commitments to men, have no need of confirmation. They are immutable, that is, unchangeable, and irrevocable: "For when God made a promise to Abraham, because He could swear by no one greater, He swore by Himself" (Heb. 6:13–14). Even subsequent divine covenants with Israel, instituted after the rescue from Egypt, do not nullify the promises to Abraham (Gal. 3:15–18). Although unnecessary, God repeatedly stated and clarified His covenant with Abraham and his descendants five times throughout Genesis (12:1–3; 13:14–17; 15:1–5; 17:1–22; 22:15–18). The multiple assurances offered to Abraham and his descendants past, present, and future have and will provide hope and encouragement in times of dark distress and doubt until the times of refreshing and the restoration of all things come (Acts 3:19–21).

EVERLASTING COVENANT

The promises of the Abrahamic Covenant give us a distinctive and everlasting path through which redemption will come and the Kingdom will be restored. This foundational covenant is not only unconditional and unchangeable, it is everlasting. Upon instituting circumcision as the sign of the covenant in Genesis 17, the Lord repeatedly called His covenant with Abraham and his descendants "everlasting" (vv. 7–8, 13, 19). King David's song of God's faithfulness when the Ark of the Covenant was placed in the Tabernacle gives praise and thanks for the Abrahamic Covenant and its everlasting promises (1 Chr. 16:17; Ps. 105:10).

LITERAL COVENANT

Lastly, the covenant promises are also to be understood as literal. To spiritualize or allegorize the descriptive terms God used to explain and confirm His word to Abraham, and then Isaac and Jacob, one must ignore the normal and common understanding of those interchanges. Abraham and his descendants took the promises literally and acted on the truth contained therein.

For example, the Promised Land is identified in Genesis 12:7; 13:14–15; 15:18–21; and 17:8. In 13:14–15 the Lord told Abram, "Lift your eyes now and look from the place where you are—northward, southward, eastward, and westward; for all the land which you see I give to you and your descendants forever." What Abram saw and what God promised was a literal, physical piece of land. Genesis 15:18 describes the literal boundaries God laid out: "On the same day the Lord made a covenant with Abram, saying: 'To your descendants I have given this land, from the river of Egypt to the great river, the River Euphrates.'"

Another example of the literalness of God's promise is Abraham's son. When God told him he would have a son with Sarah in fulfillment of the promise, Abraham laughed because he took God literally and did not understand how such an old couple could bear a son. Isaac, a literal, physical son was born (chap. 17).

J. Dwight Pentecost summarized the importance of the literal nature of the covenant promises in regard to their ultimate fulfillment:

> *Since the Abrahamic Covenant ultimately deals with Israel's title deed to the land of Palestine, her continuation as a nation to possess that land, and her redemption so that she may enjoy the blessings in the land under her King, it is of utmost importance to determine the method of the fulfillment of this covenant.*
>
> *If it is a literal covenant which needs to be fulfilled literally, then Israel must be preserved, converted, and restored. If it is an unconditional covenant, these events in Israel's national life are inevitable.*[6]

Abraham had nothing to offer to make himself worthy of such blessings. Likewise, all but One of his descendants proved unworthy as well. God sovereignly chose Abraham for a distinct purpose and covenant relationship with Him (18:19). He was called God's friend (Isa. 41:8; 2 Chr. 20:7; Jas. 2:23). Abraham was a sinner and far from perfect, but God used him greatly. Jewish scholars throughout the ages have wrestled with the moral choices and behaviors of their patriarchs. It is hard to explain Abraham's sinful and foolish choices while representing Yahweh. Who knows the extent of unnecessary difficulties that were encountered or what additional blessings may have been missed due to the disobedience of the people under the covenant? How can the promises to Abraham ultimately be fulfilled, regardless of the behaviors of the people involved? The answer lies not with the man, but with God. The unfaltering heavenly Hand of grace was there to save him and use him as a conduit for God's ultimate purposes and glory.

PROMISED REDEEMER

God's covenant with Abraham is the foundational covenant for the redemption of man, the reversal of sin's consequences, and the restoration of the theocratic Kingdom. It is in that covenant that the gospel was preached to Abraham: "And the Scripture, foreseeing that God would justify the Gentiles by faith, preached the gospel to Abraham beforehand, saying, 'In you all the nations shall be blessed'" (Gal. 3:8). It is in those promises that the plan for the coming Redeemer of Genesis 3:15 was revealed to be the Seed of Abraham (Gal. 3:16).

God did not reveal all the details of redemption's plan and the Kingdom to Abraham, Isaac, and Jacob, with whom the covenant was confirmed. As the crimson cord of redemption and golden cord of Kingdom restoration wound through the subsequent Abrahamic generations, the prophetic cues regarding the coming King, who would rule over the restoration, pointed to Jacob's son Joseph and his genetic line (Gen. 48:10). God's ultimate provision for redemption and the reversal of sin's consequences were set in motion for all people to place their faith in and follow Him like Abraham, who "believed in the LORD, and He accounted it to him for righteousness" (15:6).

The specific personal and national promises of the covenant belong to Abraham and Israel, respectively. They are God's covenant people. But within the universal promise, people who place their faith in the provision of the Redeemer Seed, Jesus Christ, receive forgiveness of sin, a place in the restored Kingdom, and the promise of eternal life (Eph. 2:12–13).

BLESSED OR CURSED

God made one more covenant promise with Abraham and the nation of Israel: "I will bless those who bless you, and I will curse him who curses you" (Gen. 12:3). This, too, is a literal and irrevocable promise.

Hebrew has two different words for *curse*. The first is used of God's promise to bring about judgment and consequences on those who oppose His people and the work He will do in and through them. The second word speaks of one who curses Abraham and his descendants, who treat them with contempt as insignificant. Modern Hebrew might translate this word as "trifle" with Abraham. The sense of the word carries the thought of treating someone in a way that diminishes and disregards God's intended purposes for them and through them. This meaning is something to consider regarding the current trend spreading in evangelical circles where Israel has been replaced and cast aside as irrelevant in God's plan for progress toward a restored Kingdom.

The purpose of the covenant is most obviously to bring blessings on Abraham, Israel, and the world. The promise to "bless those who bless you" carries great weight. God's act of elective grace in choosing Abraham and, therefore, Israel, is meant to expand the channels through which His blessings may be realized in the lives of many people. Israel has been a central figure in the divine provision of the Redeemer King, Christ the Lord, who one day will usher in the restored Kingdom, first on Earth through Israel, then for all eternity in the new heaven and new earth.

STEP OF FAITH

Abraham, like astronaut Neil Armstrong, took a giant leap for mankind; and the magnitude of the impact of his steps is yet to be fully realized. But without a doubt, God is using his footsteps to touch all of eternity.

CHAPTER FOUR

God's Kingdom and the Mosaic Covenant

Richard Schmidt

Many Gentile and Jewish people currently attempt to find peace with God through a failed effort to follow the laws and principles in the Bible. The Mosaic Law, God's conditional covenant with the nation of Israel that He gave to Moses on Mount Sinai between 1446–1445 BC[1], proved millennia ago that no one is capable of keeping God's law. In Old Testament times, God's desire was for Israel to become a "kingdom of priests and a holy nation" (Ex. 19:6). The nation of Israel was to mediate God's Word and be a blessing to other nations throughout the world. However, the Mosaic Covenant revealed mankind's sinfulness, their inability to keep the Mosaic Law, and their desperate need for a Savior (Heb. 10:1–4; Gal. 3:21–24).

To understand how the Law relates to God's coming Kingdom, this chapter examines the requirements of the Mosaic Covenant; Israel's failure to follow the covenant; Christ's fulfillment of the Mosaic Law; the abolishment of the Mosaic Covenant; and, finally, the replacement of the Mosaic Covenant with the New Covenant in the future Millennial Kingdom.

When studying the Mosaic Covenant, we need to keep in mind that it was specifically written for the Jewish people of the Old Testament period and no longer is in effect. Moral principles recorded in the Mosaic Covenant are restated in applicable Church-Age Scriptures. However, the conditional Mosaic Covenant ceased with the inauguration of the

Church Age and the gospel of God's grace (Acts 13:39; 20:24; Eph. 2:8–9).

REQUIREMENTS OF THE MOSAIC COVENANT

As we look at the relationship of the Mosaic Covenant with God's Kingdom, we first need to understand its requirements.

PEOPLE OF THE COVENANT (EXODUS 19:1–4)

The children of Israel left Canaan, journeyed to Egypt, and spent 430 years in Egypt before God delivered them from bondage under Moses' leadership (Ex. 12:40–41; Acts 7:6–7). The book of Genesis provides the historical background for the formation of the Jewish people, their time in the land of Canaan, and their choice to leave Canaan to journey to Egypt and gain relief from famine (Gen. 12:1–10; 42:5; 46:6—50:26). Egypt had experienced seven years of excellent crops, and their storehouses were full (41:29).

The children of Israel's long-term stay in Egypt eventually resulted in their bondage (Ex. 1:1–14). God knew they needed His intervention to deliver them. Therefore, He chose Moses as His first mediatorial leader in His mediatorial kingdom to deliver His Chosen People from Pharaoh (3:10).

God began the process of establishing the mediatorial kingdom when He appeared to Moses in the form of a burning bush on Mount Horeb, which is synonymous with Mount Sinai (3:1–10). God designated Moses as the first of a long line of mediatorial rulers, who would stand, or mediate, between God and the nation.[2] God miraculously delivered the children of Israel from Pharaoh and took them on a three-month journey to the Desert of Sinai (19:1), which "is called er-Raha (meaning 'the palm [of a hand]') in that it is a flat plain about 5,000 feet above sea level and stretches over 400 acres almost like an amphitheater with additional areas in adjoining valleys."[3] God spent two, four-month periods teaching Moses His commandments and laws, which Moses subsequently taught the children of Israel (24:18; 34:28; 19:3).

God promised the Israelites three benefits if they kept the commands in the Mosaic Covenant. First, God would consider them His "special treasure." Second, they would be classified as a "kingdom of priests." And third, they would comprise God's "holy nation" (19:5–6). Andrew

Woods rightly stated, "Because this is the first reference to the term 'kingdom' in relation to God's kingdom in all of the Bible, it is reasonable to conclude that the office of Theocratic Administrator that was lost in Eden was restored to the earth, at least in a limited sense, at Sinai."[4]

Alva McClain expanded on the mediatorial concept as it applied to all existing nations in Exodus 19:6:

> *The nation of Israel is to be a "kingdom of priests" (vs. 6). Now it is the main function of priests to mediate between God and men. Therefore, since all nations on earth are within the purview of the covenant, in the sense that they are to share somehow as beneficiaries of the act, the divine call of Israel must have had as one if its purposes the idea of one nation acting mediatorially in religious matters between the true God and the nations of the earth.*[5]

He went on to add an important limitation when addressing the scope of the Mosaic Law:

> *Although the law was given to Israel upon this occasion, the covenant does not set forth a way of salvation by means of law-keeping. The conditional clause qualifies the continuance of the nation of Israel in her favored position in the mediatorial kingdom of Old Testament history, functioning as God's "kingdom of priests" among the nations on earth.*[6]

Bible teachers who apply the Mosaic-Covenant mandates to people in the present Church Age contribute to doctrinal confusion. God specifically gave this covenant to Israel, the Jewish people (19:3–6; 20:3–22). The Mosaic Covenant had great value as a "teacher" for Old Testament Jewish people. However, as will be shown, Jesus' death, burial, and resurrection resulted in the dismantling of it (Gal. 3:24–26).

PRINCIPLES OF THE COVENANT (EXODUS 19:5–6)

Often the Ten Commandments are misconstrued as the entire Mosaic Law. However, there are actually 613 commandments in the Law of Moses, 365 negative and 248 positive.[7] "The Mosaic Law includes the Ten Commandments given orally to all the people, the 'book of the covenant' given to Moses alone later the same day, and the lengthy, detailed regulations revealed to Moses, again alone, during the two forty-day periods on Mt. Sinai."[8] God provided several categories of laws to the Jewish people:

Decalogue (Ex. 20:1–17)
The Ten Commandments, or Decalogue, comprise the most commonly known section of the Mosaic Covenant. The term comes from Exodus 34:27–28: "Then the LORD said to Moses, 'Write these words, for according to the tenor of these words I have made a covenant with you and with Israel.' So he was there with the LORD forty days and forty nights; he neither ate bread nor drank water. And He wrote on the tablets the words of the covenant, the Ten Commandments."

God reiterated the importance of the Decalogue in Deuteronomy 4:13: "So He declared to you His covenant which He commanded you to perform, the Ten Commandments; and He wrote them on two tablets of stone." "These 'ten words' were distinguished from the rest of the law of God in that they were audibly delivered to Moses by God Himself and later written by God on tablets of stone."[9]

Book of the Covenant (Ex. 20:22—23:33)
Immediately after God stressed the importance of the Ten Commandments, He commanded Moses to teach the children of Israel the more than 600 other specific commandments and laws (Dt. 4:14). God sovereignly designed the Mosaic Covenant to reveal to the Israelites that following the Law was humanly impossible. The covenant pointed out the sinful weakness of mankind. Therefore, God required blood sacrifices to make atonement for sin, or, better stated, to cover sin (Lev. 17:11).[10] The Mosaic Covenant condemned sinful mankind, but God provided the ultimate sacrifice when sending Jesus Christ, His Son, to Earth in a virgin-born, human body to willingly die and pay the penalty for condemned men and women (Rom. 5:6–8; 1 Cor. 15:3–4).

The Book of the Covenant provided the Jewish people and proselytes to Judaism with specific laws they were to follow as a society. The Mosaic Law contained the principles to govern the nation; and, therefore, the three main categories of religious, moral, and civil laws made perfect sense in providing guidance for God's historical kingdom.[11] Since explaining each category of laws would require a large volume, I'll summarize them to provide a basic guideline of the details God included in the Law.

God directed Moses to write His laws regarding the proper conduct of His people in dealing with others and the penalties for violating the laws. Moses recorded the laws concerning the treatment of slaves (Ex. 21:1–11), murderers (vv. 12–17), those who inflicted bodily injury on another person (vv. 18–32), and people who caused property damage to another person (21:33—22:15).

God also mandated specific laws for the Jewish nation regarding the penalties for violating a virgin (22:16–17), practicing sorcery (v. 18), bestiality (v. 19), making idolatrous sacrifices (v. 20), mistreatment of foreigners (v. 21), and maltreatment of widows and orphans (vv. 22–24). The Law also addressed charging interest on loans (vv. 25–27), blasphemy against God and cursing rulers (v. 28), firstfruits that must be offered to God (vv. 29–30), and the importance of maintaining holiness, which included not eating meat killed by beasts (v. 31).[12]

The next major category of laws regarded appropriate conduct with neighbors (23:1–9). Moses recorded laws concerning not spreading false reports (v. 1), avoiding groups bent on evil (v. 2), giving prejudicial testimony (vv. 3, 6), returning stray animals to owners (v. 4), preserving the lives of the innocent and righteous (v. 7), refusing to take a bribe (v. 8), and the proper treatment of strangers (v. 9).[13]

The final major category in this section addresses "laws on sacred seasons" (vv. 10–19). The subcategories include keeping land Sabbaths (vv. 10–11) and keeping the weekly Sabbath (v. 12). Moses recorded additional commands, including never mentioning false gods (v. 13) and keeping three specific feasts: Feast of Unleavened Bread, Feast of Harvest, and Feast of Ingathering (vv. 15–17). Moses closed the section with commands regarding sacrifices, firstfruits of the land, and forbidding the boiling of a goat in its mother's milk (v. 19).[14]

The remainder of the book of Exodus addresses the proper worship of God. Based on the length and detail of the narrative, it stresses the importance of properly approaching and worshiping God (chaps. 25—40).

Moses warned the children of Israel that receiving God's blessings was contingent on them keeping the commandments in the Mosaic Covenant (23:20–33). The covenant stood in contrast to the Abrahamic (Gen 12:1–3), Land (Dt. 30:1–10), Davidic (2 Sam 7:12–16), and New

(Jer. 31:31–40) Covenants, which had unconditional blessings. Instead, the Mosaic Covenant set strict conditions the children of Israel had to follow, or they would forfeit God's blessing.

The New Testament clearly states that a person can only be "justified by faith in Christ and not by the works of the law; for by the works of the law no flesh shall be justified" (Gal. 2:16). God provided the children of Israel with a covering for sin through the sacrificial system described in the Mosaic Law (Lev. 4:20–35; Heb. 10:4–11). Christ's First Advent provided the ultimate sacrifice that took away the effects of sin through His death, burial, and resurrection (Heb. 7:27; 9:12–28; 10:10).

PURPOSE OF THE COVENANT (EXODUS 19:7–8)

There are multiple reasons why God instituted the Mosaic Covenant:
1. The Mosaic Law revealed God's holiness (1 Pet. 1:5–16).
2. The Law clearly exposed man's sinful nature (Rom. 3:23; Gal.3:19–23).
3. The Law revealed God's standard to maintain a right relationship with Himself (Ps. 24:3–5).
4. God used the Law as a schoolmaster to lead people to Jesus Christ (Ps. 119:71–72; Gal. 3:24).
5. God provided the Law as the national constitution for the children of Israel (Ex. 19:5–8; Dt. 28).
6. The Law provided the guidelines for Israel to become a kingdom of priests and act as mediators between God and the nations (Ex. 19:5–6; 31:13).
7. The Law provided the provision to cover sin, resulting in restored fellowship with God (Lev. 1—7).
8. The Mosaic Law revealed God's provision for His people to worship Him through the annual feasts (Lev. 23).
9. God provided important tests to reveal if a person was part of His kingdom (Dt. 28).
10. The Mosaic Law prepared the people for the coming Messiah (Mt. 24:25–27).[15]

FAILURE OF THE MOSAIC COVENANT

God instituted the Mosaic Covenant to vividly reveal the sinfulness of the children of Israel and their complete inability to follow His commandments (Rom. 5:20; Gal. 3:11). The Jewish people and all Gentiles were in the hopeless state of condemnation under the Mosaic Law. The sacrificial system provided a covering for sin (Lev.16:32–34), but the outright disobedience of the children of Israel placed them in an unacceptable relationship with God.

The Lord is aware there is nothing inherently good in man since sin entered the world through Adam's transgression (Gen 3:6–7; Rom. 5:12). All men and woman inherited the sin nature as a result of Adam's sin. God knew that no human being was capable of 100 percent compliance with the Mosaic Law. Therefore, God in His mercy provided the timely remedy not only to cover sin, but to remove the effects and condemnation associated with sin.

FULFILLMENT OF THE MOSAIC COVENANT

God's timing is always perfect, and His redemptive plan is no exception. The apostle Paul wrote in several epistles about the timeliness of Christ's coming not only to personally fulfill the Mosaic Law (cf. Mt. 5:17) but to abolish the Old Covenant and provide eternal life to all who by faith accept Christ's atoning work.

Man has no strength to save himself, but "in due time Christ died for the ungodly" (Rom. 5:6). This concept is expanded in Galatians 4:4–5: "But when the fullness of the time had come, God sent forth His Son, born of a woman, born under the law, to redeem those who were under the law, that we might receive the adoption as sons." Paul made the perfect summary statement in Galatians 2:16: "Knowing that a man is not justified by the works of the law [Mosaic Law] but by faith in Jesus Christ, even we have believed in Christ Jesus, that we might be justified by faith in Christ and not by the works of the law; for by the works of the law no flesh shall be justified." Jesus Christ is the only One who could completely follow and fulfill the Mosaic Law as the sinless Savior.

ABOLISHMENT OF THE MOSAIC LAW (GALATIANS 3:23—4:7)

The Mosaic Law, with emphatic certainty, is no longer in effect. It was temporary and stands in stark contrast to the gospel of God's grace, which was realized through Jesus Christ's death, burial, and resurrection (1 Cor. 15:3–4; Eph. 2:8–9; Ti. 3:5–6). The Mosaic Law had no ability to justify sinful man with the righteous God (Gal. 2:16; 3:11, 21; Heb. 10:4); it confined everyone to bondage (Gal. 4:1–4).

Under the Holy Spirit's inspiration (2 Tim. 3:16), the apostle Paul wrote the letter to the Christians at Galatia to encourage them to stand firm in their liberty from the Law, which they received when they trusted in the gospel of God's grace. Paul denounced people who were pressuring Christians to return to following the Mosaic Law, stating this reason: "The law was our tutor to bring us to Christ, that we might be justified by faith. But after faith has come, we are no longer under a tutor. For you are all sons of God through faith in Christ Jesus" (Gal. 3:24–26). J. Dwight Pentecost provided insight into the concept of a tutor, or schoolmaster:

> *In Greek society the schoolmaster was responsible for the oversight of the family heir in every area of his life. The Law was designed to be a schoolmaster for Israel to control every area of the people's lives. They as God's children were not responsible to make decisions—their decisions were made for them by the Law. Their only responsibility then was to put themselves under its authority as a schoolmaster and to obey.*[16]

REPLACEMENT OF THE MOSAIC COVENANT

Christ abolished the Mosaic Covenant, but He also instituted the New Covenant still to come.

The prophet Jeremiah revealed that God will institute this covenant specifically with the house of Israel and the house of Judah. It will not mimic the conditional Mosaic Covenant (Jer. 31:32) but will provide unconditional benefits for the Jewish people. Jeremiah revealed that God's New Covenant will produce a positive relationship with the Jewish people: "I will put My law in their minds, and write it on their hearts; I will be their God, and they shall be My people (Jer. 31:33).

The New Covenant, like the Abrahamic, Land, and Davidic Covenants, provides unconditional future blessings for the Jewish people. The literal fulfillment of the stated covenants will occur during Jesus Christ's yet future Second Advent and establishment of His theocratic, Millennial Kingdom on Earth (Rev. 19:11—20:6). The New Covenant guarantees the Jewish people's eternal existence coupled with God's blessings (Jer. 31:31–34). God will literally change the hearts and minds of the Jewish people during His prophesied earthly Kingdom, thus enabling Israel to obey God.[17]

CONCLUSION

God designed the Mosaic Covenant, with its conditional promises, to prove that the children of Israel would never be able to keep the 613 commandments. And He provided the Jewish people and Gentile proselytes with the sacrificial system to cover their sins until the ultimate and once-for-all sacrifice of Jesus Christ at His First Coming (Heb. 10:1–10). His death resulted in the abolishment of the Mosaic Law.

Today we look forward to the Second Coming of the Lord Jesus Christ when He returns to inaugurate His 1,000-year, Millennial Kingdom on Earth (Rev. 19:11—20:6). God will then institute His Abrahamic, Land, Davidic, and New Covenants with the children of Israel.

What a glorious time that will be!

CHAPTER FIVE

God's Kingdom and the Davidic Covenant

Tom Simcox

Have you ever been so grateful for something someone did for you that you wanted desperately to be able to reciprocate? You wanted to say "Thank you" in a tangible way to show your extreme appreciativeness.

That was how King David felt. His heart was so full of joy and gratitude to God for all the Lord had done for him that he wanted to build God a house, a magnificent Temple in which the Almighty would dwell.

But God had other plans. His plans did not involve a house for Himself but, rather, a house for David. He would do more for the young king than David ever imagined. From David's seed, God promised to establish a Kingdom of righteousness that would endure forever. That seed and Kingdom are the central components of what has become known as the Davidic Covenant.

DAVID'S BACKGROUND

David must have appeared an unlikely recipient of such a divine promise—at least to his family. The youngest of Jesse's eight sons, his job growing up was to tend the sheep. He probably spent many hours alone in the fields with the flock, contemplating the wonders of creation and his insignificance before such a magnificent Creator (Ps. 8:3–5). Sensitive and artistic, David played the harp and composed songs. In fact, his brothers apparently stereotyped him as a typical Israelite shepherd—a dreamer, whose opinion no one valued and whose testimony was even inadmissible in court. Shepherds were considered the lowest class of Israelite society.

God, of course, doesn't think as we do. He chooses "the foolish things of the world to put to shame the wise," and "the weak things of the world to put to shame the things that are mighty...that no flesh should glory in His presence" (1 Cor. 1:27, 29). To his family, David looked foolish and inconsequential. But to God he was "a man after My own heart" (Acts 13:22). In his service as a shepherd, David's faith grew as he often needed to protect his flock from predators. The Lord used all his experiences tending sheep to prepare him for service as shepherd over God's nation, Israel.

David's family thought so little of him that when the prophet Samuel arrived in Bethlehem, looking for the man God wanted him to anoint as king of Israel to replace Saul, no one even bothered to get the youth from the field. It wasn't until the Lord rejected all of David's brothers that Samuel asked, "Are all the young men here?" (1 Sam. 16:11).

Jesse replied, "There remains yet the youngest, and there he is, keeping the sheep" (v. 11). When David appeared, the Lord told Samuel, "Arise, anoint him; for this is the one!" (v. 12). God took David as a teenager from the sheepfold, strengthened his faith, saved his life many times when a crazed and jealous King Saul tried to kill him, and installed him as king over all Israel at age 30.

DESIRE AND DECLARATION

What could David possibly do to express his thanks to God and honor Him for all He had done for the man? As the psalmist wrote, "What shall I render to the LORD for all His benefits toward me?" (Ps. 116:12). David's deepest desire was to build the Lord a Temple:

> *Now it came to pass when the king was dwelling in his house, and the LORD had given him rest from all his enemies all around, that the king said to Nathan the prophet, "See now, I dwell in a house of cedar, but the ark of God dwells inside tent curtains." Then Nathan said to the king, "Go, do all that is in your heart, for the LORD is with you"* (2 Sam. 7:1–3).

GOD'S KINGDOM AND THE DAVIDIC COVENANT

Neither Nathan nor David understood the magnitude of God's plan, which is so far-reaching it affects all of humanity. So that night, the Lord told Nathan what to tell David:

> *Thus says the L*ORD*: "Would you build a house for Me to dwell in? For I have not dwelt in a house since the time that I brought the children of Israel up from Egypt, even to this day, but have moved about in a tent and in a tabernacle. Wherever I have moved about with all the children of Israel, have I ever spoken a word to anyone from the tribes of Israel, whom I commanded to shepherd My people Israel, saying, 'Why have you not built Me a house of cedar?' Now therefore, thus shall you say to My servant David, 'Thus says the L*ORD *of hosts: "I took you from the sheepfold, from following the sheep, to be ruler over My people, over Israel. And I have been with you wherever you have gone, and have cut off all your enemies from before you, and have made you a great name, like the name of the great men who are on the earth. Moreover I **will appoint a place for My people Israel, and will plant them, that they may dwell in a place of their own and move no more**; nor shall the sons of wickedness oppress them anymore, as previously, since the time that I commanded judges to be over My people Israel, and have caused you to rest from all your enemies. Also the L*ORD *tells you that He will make you a house.*
>
> *"When your days are fulfilled and you rest with your fathers, **I will set up your seed after you**, who will come from your body, **and I will establish his kingdom**. He shall build a house for My name, and **I will establish the throne of his kingdom forever**. I will be his Father, and he shall be My son. If he commits iniquity, I will chasten him with the rod of men and with the blows of the sons of men. But My mercy shall not depart from him, as I took it from Saul, whom I removed from before you. **And your house and your kingdom shall be established forever** before you. Your throne shall be established forever"* (vv. 5–16, emphasis added).

The patriarch Jacob had already prophesied that Israel's Messiah would come from the tribe of Judah: "The scepter shall not depart from Judah, nor a lawgiver from between his feet, until Shiloh come;

and to Him shall be the obedience of the people" (Gen. 49:10). Now, through the Davidic Covenant, God identified the precise family in Judah through which the Messiah would come: King David's.

God always gives us progressive revelation. He unfolds His plan a little at a time. Everything builds on itself as He unveils how He intends to bring about what He promised. The themes of a Kingdom and a Redeemer have been running through the Bible since the book of Genesis, but with David they became more precise.

Through the Davidic Covenant, God made five key declarations involving His people, His Redeemer, and His Kingdom:

1. "I will appoint a place for My people Israel, and will plant them, that they may dwell in a place of their own and move no more."
2. "I will set up your seed after you."
3. "I will establish his kingdom."
4. "I will establish the throne of his kingdom forever."
5. "Your house and your kingdom shall be established forever."

DAVIDIC COVENANT TERMS

Let's look at these five declarations in more detail.

PLACE FOR ISRAEL

God promised to establish Israel in the Promised Land forever, reaffirming the covenant He made with Abraham (Gen. 17:1–8); Abraham's son Isaac (26:3); Isaac's son Jacob (28:13); and, finally, Jacob's descendants (35:12). Throughout the Old Testament, God continually reiterates His intent to bring the Jewish people back to their own land and establish them on the hills of Israel. One such clear prophecy appears in the book of Ezekiel: "Thus says the Lord God: 'I will gather you from the peoples, assemble you from the countries where you have been scattered, and I will give you the land of Israel'" (11:17).

This promise, by its nature, guarantees Jewry's existence because it assures David that no matter how horribly the world treats the Jewish people, God will make sure they return to their land and live there in peace. David received this promise hundreds of years before either the Assyrian or Babylonian Captivities and more than 2,000 years before the Holocaust, which almost exterminated all of European Jewry. It is quite a promise! No other nation in history has that ironclad guarantee that it will exist forever.

ROYAL SEED

The Davidic Covenant's promise of seed is twofold: (1) It involves David's immediate heirs, namely, Solomon and the kings of Judah. (2) It also looks to a time when a seed (descendant) of David's will rule forever. That Seed, of course, is the divine Messiah, Jesus.

About 1,000 years after God made this promise to David, the angel Gabriel harkened back to it when he told Mary, a direct descendant of the king, "Behold, you will conceive in your womb and bring forth a Son, and shall call His name Jesus. He will be great, and will be called the Son of the Highest; and the Lord God will give Him the throne of His father David. And He will reign over the house of Jacob forever, and of His kingdom there will be no end" (Lk. 1:31–33).

Gabriel also echoed the prophet Isaiah, who said,

For unto us a Child is born, unto us a Son is given; and the government will be upon His shoulder. And His name will be called Wonderful, Counselor, Mighty God, Everlasting Father, Prince of Peace. Of the increase of His government and peace there will be no end, upon the throne of David and over His kingdom, to order it and establish it with judgment and justice from that time forward, even forever. The zeal of the LORD of hosts will perform this (Isa. 9:6–7).

Many other passages allude to the Davidic Covenant. Psalm 132:11 is among the most compelling: "The LORD has sworn in truth to David; He will not turn from it: 'I will set upon your throne the fruit of your body.'"

ENDURING KINGDOM

This promised Seed of David's will rule over a restored Jewish kingdom and the world, as the prophet Daniel explained to Babylonian King Nebuchadnezzar: "The God of heaven will set up a kingdom which shall never be destroyed; and the kingdom shall not be left to other people; it shall break in pieces and consume all these [Gentile] kingdoms, and it shall stand forever" (Dan. 2:44).

We need to understand that there is a huge difference between the Millennial Kingdom and the eternal Kingdom. In the Millennial Kingdom, Jesus will sit on a throne in Jerusalem and rule from there for 1,000 years. Although that's an incomprehensibly long time to us, it nevertheless is finite. It comes to an end. However, when the Millennial Kingdom ends, the eternal Kingdom begins. And Messiah Jesus will rule that Kingdom forever: "And there were loud voices in heaven, saying, 'The kingdoms of this world have become the kingdoms of our Lord and of His Christ, and He shall reign forever and ever!'" (Rev. 11:15).

To quote Bible expositor David M. Levy, "Christ's realm is David's kingdom forever" (Lk. 1:33).

EVERLASTING THRONE AND HOUSE

By promising to establish the throne of David's kingdom forever, God was declaring that the right to rule would remain with David's descendants for all time. They and they alone would be the legitimate sovereigns.

When the united kingdom of Israel became divided under King Solomon's son Rehoboam, the ten northern tribes became known as Israel; and the two southern tribes of Benjamin and Judah became known as Judah. Only the kings of Judah were Davidic kings. God faithfully preserved David's line and saw to it that each Davidic king was a legitimate heir to the throne. Each had the right to rule.

Shortly before the Babylonian Captivity, the Lord became so enraged with Judean King Jeconiah (also called Coniah) that He declared through the prophet Jeremiah,

> *"As I live," says the* Lord, *"though Coniah the son of Jehoiakim, king of Judah, were the signet on My right hand, yet I would pluck you off; and I will give you into the hand of those who seek your life."*

> *Thus says the* Lord: *"Write this man down as childless, a man who shall not prosper in his days; for none of his descendants shall prosper, sitting on the throne of David, and ruling anymore in Judah"* (Jer. 22:24–25, 30).

It would appear that, from this point on, any king who descended from Solomon's line basically would be cursed. He would never prosper on David's throne. But we know for certain that Jesus will indeed prosper and have the legal right to rule forever. How can this be? Because in His humanity, Jesus descended from David's son Nathan through His mother, Mary, rather than through Solomon (Lk. 3:23, 31). Yet He obtained the legal right to rule from His stepfather, Joseph, who was David's direct heir through Solomon (Mt. 1:1–6, 16).

Solomon, of course, sinned against God by marrying many foreign women and worshiping their idols. Yet the Lord promised David that even if his descendants sinned, He would never remove the throne from David's line, as He did with Saul. David's seed would have the legal authority to rule forever.

The word *house* in 2 Samuel 7:16 refers to a dynasty. David's dynasty will continue for eternity—not Solomon's, but David's.

PERMANENT ESTABLISHMENT

The Davidic Covenant stresses permanency. Nothing can alter God's plan. The promises He made to David are unconditional, unbreakable, and unalterable. There is probably no stronger statement in all of Scripture to attest to this fact than Psalm 89:

> *I have made a covenant with My chosen, I have sworn to My servant David: "Your seed I will establish forever, and build up your throne to all generations"* (3–4).

> *My mercy I will keep for him forever, and My covenant shall stand firm with him. His seed also I will make to endure forever, and his throne as the days of heaven. If his sons forsake My law and do not walk in My judgments, if they break My statutes and do not keep My commandments, then I will punish their transgression with the rod, and their iniquity with stripes. Nevertheless My lovingkindness I will not utterly take from him, nor allow My faithfulness to fail. My covenant I will not break, nor alter the word that has gone out of My lips. Once I have sworn by My holiness; I will not lie to David: His seed shall endure forever, and his throne as the sun before Me; it shall be established forever like the moon, even like the faithful witness in the sky* (vv. 28–37).

HOPE FOR US TODAY

As we look at all that is happening in the world today, it's easy to become depressed. Evil is everywhere, and good seems to be nowhere. But we must take heart because we serve a God with absolute power who is unequivocally faithful. He promised that, from David's seed, He will establish a Kingdom of righteousness that will endure forever. He also will establish the Jewish people in their land, where they never again will suffer affliction. We need to keep our eyes on Him and know that what He said, He will do; and no one will reverse it (Isa. 43:13).

CHAPTER SIX

God's Kingdom Anticipation in the First Century

Mike Stallard

Christians look forward to God's Kingdom for a variety of reasons. Some want relief from physical suffering, while others want to escape schedules and deadlines. Some want to be reunited with family members and friends who have died and spend time with them. Others want to live without temptation and sin. And the list of reasons goes on, whether they are scripturally accurate or not.

In Jesus' day, the Jewish people looked forward to God's Kingdom, too, although what they expected was a political Kingdom, not the Kingdom Old Testament prophets described.

In the first century, the Jewish people had been under the oppressive yoke of the Roman Empire since 63 BC. Before that, they suffered foreign domination under the Babylonians, Persians, and Greeks, as Daniel described in his prophecies of the sixth century BC. Judea had a brief reprieve when the Maccabean revolt brought Jewish independence under the Hasmoneans, beginning in the second century BC. But self-rule ended when Rome asserted its power in the region.

Through all this time, the Jewish hope of a coming Messiah to set up an earthly Kingdom was a never-dying hope. They eagerly anticipated a day when Messiah would come to Earth and make all things right in His Kingdom. What was the basis of their hope?

OLD TESTAMENT PROMISES OF THE KINGDOM

The Jewish people of the first century could find such hope in the literal teachings of the Old Testament. Taken at face value, the most often-presented idea of the Kingdom in the Old Testament is an earthly Kingdom initiated by God through Messiah, the ultimate King of Israel. The tone for an earthly Kingdom is set as early as the book of Job: "I know that my Redeemer lives, and He shall stand at last on the earth" (Job 19:25).

The Kingdom teaching of the Old Testament stems from the great biblical covenants: Abrahamic (Gen. 12; 15; 17), Davidic (2 Sam. 7; Ps. 89), and New (Jer. 31). In the Abrahamic Covenant, God granted the deed to the land of Israel to Abraham and his descendants forever. In the Davidic Covenant, He promised the throne of the Kingdom of Israel to the descendants of David forever. An ultimate and final son of David, Christ, will rule and reign forever, not only for a thousand years. In the New Covenant, God promised a spiritual restoration of Israel in the end-times. Often forgotten is that such ultimate spiritual restoration involves Israel being a nation forever (Jer. 31:31–37).

Specific predictions and promises in the Old Testament related to the end-times Kingdom for Israel are numerous. For example, in Amos 9:15 God said of His people Israel, "I will plant them in their land, and no longer shall they be pulled up from the land I have given them." This positive prophecy was given in the eighth century BC during the time of the divided kingdom and promised an ultimate and permanent unification of the nation.

In the same century, the prophet Isaiah gave frequent prophecies about Israel's coming Kingdom, although he may be known more for his prediction of the Messiah's death (fulfilled in the First Coming of Jesus Christ) as an atonement for sin (Isa. 53). For example, Isaiah 9:6–7, the beautiful and well-known passage about Messiah, also forecasts the Kingdom:

> *For unto us a Child is born, unto us a Son is given; and the government will be upon His shoulder. And His name will be called Wonderful, Counselor, Mighty God, Everlasting Father, Prince of Peace. Of the increase of His government and peace, there will be no end, upon the throne of David and over His kingdom, to order it and establish*

it with judgment and justice from that time forward even forever.

Although this passage refers to Jesus' birth, it also alludes to the future work of the divine Messiah to reign on the throne of David forever. The passage is political as well as spiritual. There is a coming, earthly Kingdom where Christ will execute His rule without end.

Another example of Isaiah's prophecies about the Kingdom is in chapter 11, which shows three aspects of it in a passage that most likely refers to the Millennium. First, there is Messiah's presence on Earth, ruling with a rod of iron and righteousness (vv. 1–5). Second, there are massive changes in nature, such as the wolf dwelling with the lamb (vv. 6–9). Third, a restored Israel, gathered from the entire world, becomes the center of Messiah's worldwide Kingdom as the nations seek the Lord in Israel (vv. 10–16; cf. 2:1–4). Such a portrait would certainly give hope to the people of Israel for their national and spiritual future.

In addition, the prophet Jeremiah, who served the Lord just before the Babylonian Captivity and in its early years, told the Israelites not to despair since they will one day possess the land of Israel again (Jer. 32:12–15). The Branch, or Messianic King from the line of David, will one day come on the scene to execute righteousness in the context of a restoration of Jerusalem and Israel (33:15–17).

Likewise, the exilic prophet Ezekiel spoke of future Kingdom restoration for the nation:

I will take the children of Israel from among the nations, wherever they have gone, and will gather them from every side and bring them into their own land; and I will make them one nation in the land, on the mountains of Israel; and one king shall be king over them all; they shall no longer be two nations.

Then they shall dwell in the land that I have given to Jacob My servant, where your fathers dwelt; and they shall dwell there, they, their children, and their children's children, forever (Ezek. 37:21–22, 25).

Perhaps the most stunning Old Testament prophecies of the Kingdom are found in Daniel. Chapters 2 and 7 both predict a succession of four world empires: Babylon, Medo-Persia, Greece, and Rome. There is evidence that the last empire, Rome, is not only the first-century Rome of the New Testament but also an end-times version of that empire. The prophecies of Daniel take the reader all the way to a time of individual resurrection, a clear end-times event (Dan. 12:2). Furthermore, Daniel 7 speaks of the Son of Man coming to the Ancient of Days to receive a Kingdom (vv. 13–14). Not only is this a Kingdom that endures forever, its character is earthly like the preceding four kingdoms.

This Kingdom comes when the Son of Man, the Messiah, comes at the time of the destruction of the little horn, or leader of the fourth world empire in the last days. This little horn corresponds to the Antichrist, or Beast, who is destroyed at the Second Coming of Christ in Revelation 19. The Kingdom, according to Daniel 7, begins after the little horn persecutes the saints for three and a half years, the last half of the Tribulation period (v. 25; cf. Mt. 24:21). The Son of Man in Daniel 7 became the fountain for Messianic hope in the intertestamental period from Malachi to Matthew.[1]

Such Old Testament predictions, only some of which I've cited here, produced in the people of Israel a longing for the coming of Messiah in the same way that Christians today eagerly watch for the Second Coming of Jesus. It was this anticipation of a coming Kingdom that was in the air, so to speak, when the events of the New Testament began to take place.

JOHN THE BAPTIST AND THE PREACHING OF THE KINGDOM

The Gospels of Mark and Luke begin with significant narratives concerning John the Baptist. Matthew discussed this important person, as well, when Jesus talked to the crowd about John while the prophet was in prison (Mt. 11:7–10). All three Gospels allude to the prediction from Malachi 3:1: "Behold, I send My messenger, and he will prepare the way before Me" (Mt. 11:10; Mk. 1:2; Lk. 7:27). In addition, all four Gospels mention the prophecy of Isaiah 40:3—"The voice of one crying in the wilderness: 'Prepare the way of the Lord'"—as fulfilled in the ministry of John the Baptist (Mt. 3:3; Mk. 1:3; Lk. 3:4; Jn. 1:23).

Three main aspects of John's ministry characterized him as preparing the way for the First Coming of the Messiah. First, he was the one who baptized Jesus in the Jordan River (Mk. 1:9–11). John himself noted that he only baptized people using water, but the Messiah was coming to baptize with the Holy Spirit and fire (Mt. 3:11–12). By allowing John to baptize him, Jesus identified with the message of John, which pointed to Jesus as the Messiah who would take away the sin of the world (Jn. 1:29).

Second, John preached a "baptism of repentance for the remission of sins" (Mk. 1:4; Lk. 3:3). In light of the anticipation that the Messiah would come soon, the Jewish people should be prepared. They should repent (change their thinking about their sin) and admit their need to be saved. Thus, John commanded the Jewish people who came to him to confess their sins (agree with God about them); be baptized in water as a symbol of cleansing from sin; and, at times, demonstrate that repentance had taken place before being baptized (Mt. 3:5–9; Mk. 1:4–5). However, John's baptism was not the same as Christian baptism since the apostle Paul later asked disciples of John the Baptist to update their faith and be baptized in the name of Jesus, in spite of the fact that they had already been baptized by John (Acts 19:1–7).

The third way that John prepared for Christ's First Coming into the world—perhaps the most important one—was preaching: "Repent, for the kingdom of heaven is at hand!" (Mt. 3:2). The "kingdom of heaven" does not refer to God's rule in heaven, His abode. Sometimes it is thought that the Kingdom of heaven and the Kingdom of God are two different things. While it is true that there are differences between God's rule in heaven and on Earth, that is not what Matthew was talking about.

He wrote primarily with Jewish people in mind, especially those who had come to faith in Christ. So he used the term *heaven* in place of the word *God*, which is common in Jewish culture. Therefore, in Christ's teaching in the Gospel of Matthew, Kingdom of heaven means the same as Kingdom of God. In Matthew 19:23–24, Jesus used the terms interchangeably when He spoke of the difficulty of a rich man entering the Kingdom of heaven, or Kingdom of God. Also, the parallel passages in the other Gospels show that the two terms are interchangeable. (See Matthew 13:11 and Mark 4:11.)

Both terms highlight the earthly expectation of a restored nation in the end-times. The Messiah was coming, but so was the Kingdom. Jewish people in the first century expected the Messiah to throw off the Roman oppression and fulfill the Old Testament predictions of restoring Israel and ruling on the throne of David. They were not longing for a spiritual kingdom in the heart, nor did they believe only in God's general sovereignty over all things. While it is good to long for God's rule in one's inner being and believe God is the Boss of the universe, they were looking for something else: specific fulfillment of political deliverance and the rule of Messiah as envisioned in Isaiah 9:6–7 and other passages.

Such a political deliverance was, according to John, "at hand." These words convey the idea that the concrete, earthly Kingdom is overhanging, imminent, impending, and available when the Messiah comes. It is at the door. Once He comes, it is possible to establish this worldwide Kingdom centered in Israel. Some interpreters are tempted to see this expression fulfilled in Jesus' First Advent and the Kingdom as referring to a spiritual one, rather than an earthly one.

It is false to say that an earthly, political view of the Kingdom is carnal and not spiritual in any way. The Lord's ways of righteousness will dominate the earthly, political Kingdom of Israel and the world when Jesus comes again. However, the message of John the Baptist required a response on the part of the people. The establishment of the Kingdom was not automatic in the first century, even though the people had high expectations.

JESUS AND THE PREACHING OF THE KINGDOM

After Jesus was baptized by John, He endured the devil's temptations (Mt. 4:1–11), He began His preaching ministry. Jesus' favorite designation for Himself was "Son of Man," taken from the picture of the Messianic King in Daniel 7. Christ's message was the same as John the Baptist's: "Repent, for the kingdom of heaven is at hand" (Mt. 4:17). The kingdom was "in your midst" (Lk. 17:21 NASB)[2] in the person of Christ the King.

Because the King was present on Earth, the fulfillment of all the Old Testament promises for the restoration of Israel in Kingdom glory was now possible. Jesus' preaching in this sense was what can legitimately be called an offer of the Kingdom. The people of Israel had to repent and accept Jesus as their Messianic King for the earthly Kingdom to be initiated and Roman rule overthrown. Sadly, only a relative minority accepted Jesus as their Messiah, so the apostle John decades later penned these words: "He came to His own, and His own did not receive Him" (Jn. 1:11).

Israel's rejection of Jesus led to a delay in setting up the Kingdom, sometimes called the postponement of the Kingdom. The delay is from the point of view of Israel's anticipation of the Kingdom in the first century and not from God's point of view. God knows the beginning from the end. He is sovereign over history, and Jewish rejection of Jesus did not take the Lord by surprise.

Yet detractors of this view sometimes ridicule such an understanding. Pastor G. I. Williamson commented negatively on it: "The Messiah came and offered to establish this kingdom. The Jews refused. Christ was therefore forced to delay the establishment of the Kingdom. He temporarily withdrew (going into a far country, Matt. 21:33) but will return to do what he was then kept from doing."[3] Such wording makes it appear that those who believe in an offer of the Kingdom followed by a delay due to rejection are attacking the sovereignty of God and making Jesus to be a pawn blown around by human decisions. This is a caricature of the dispensational position of postponement of the Kingdom.

In response to the charge, notice that at the triumphal entry, Jesus' followers were hailing Him as King of Israel and no doubt wanted Him at that time to overthrow the Romans (Lk. 19:28–40). The realistic nature of their hope came through the miracles Jesus had done. Only such a miracle worker could defeat the Romans.

What many interpreters miss is the parable of the minas that Jesus told His audience just before His triumphal entry (Lk. 19:11–27). In fact, He gave them this parable "because He was near Jerusalem and because they thought the kingdom of God would appear immediately" (v. 11). The parable tells of a nobleman (Christ) who goes into a far country to receive authority to return to the land and rule. The point of the teaching is that the Kingdom was going to be delayed from the vantage point of the expectations of those who wanted Him to begin His rule right away. The Kingdom was going to come later (at Christ's Second Coming). Hence, the idea of a delay or postponement in the Kingdom is a biblical teaching.

This arrangement is analogous to the time when Joshua sent twelve spies into the Promised Land (Num. 13). God brought the children of Israel to Kadesh in the Wilderness of Paran as they prepared to enter and possess the land promised to their father Abraham. When the spies came back, ten of the twelve gave a negative report that the land could not be conquered. As a result, the congregation on the whole rejected God's plan to enter into Canaan to take the land (Num. 14). The consequence of their rejection was forty years of wandering in the wilderness.

After the forty years, God finally allowed the nation to possess the land. One way to describe this order of events is that possession of the land was delayed or postponed by forty years. Did this mean God's original plan for the Israelites to enter the land was thwarted? Does such a sequence of events prove God is not sovereign? Not at all.

The delay did not catch God by surprise. Neither did the first-century rejection of Jesus by the Jewish people and the consequent delay in establishing God's earthly Kingdom. The anticipation of the Jews for a Kingdom in the first century was not fulfilled.

JESUS AND THE DELAYED KINGDOM

Were the people of Israel in the first century mistaken for expecting a Messiah to come and set up an earthly Kingdom where national Israel is restored? The answer is clear: "The nation was not rejected [by God] because they had a wrong concept of the kingdom, but because they failed to repent. Jesus was not attempting to change their ideas of an earthly kingdom; rather He was attempting to bring them to the place where they might obtain it."[4] In the end, their rejection led them to be wrong about the *timing* of the establishment of the kingdom.

Why did they fail to identify Jesus as the long-awaited Messiah? While some accepted Him as their Messiah, most did not think Jesus fit the part. They expected a Messiah to come in glory to reign over the nation as many Old Testament passages predicted. But many people overlooked the Old Testament verses that taught something else about Messiah, namely, His death.

Isaiah 53 gives a portrait of a suffering, individual Messiah who would be afflicted, chastised, and crushed for our sins. "He was cut off from the land of the living" (v. 8). Daniel 9:26 also states that Messiah will be "cut off," or killed. A Messiah portrayed in such passages was of no immediate help to throw off the chains of the Roman Empire. As a result, such teaching gathered little support in the first century because of the expectations of the times.[5]

The question confronting Israel was this: "How could Jesus be the Messiah since He was killed on the cross?" The answer is Christ's resurrection from the dead. The Old Testament looked ahead to this resurrection in Psalm 16:10: "For You will not leave my soul in Sheol, nor will You allow Your Holy One to see corruption." Peter's sermon on the day of Pentecost made use of this prediction to argue that Jesus can and will serve as the coming Messianic King of Israel because He had been raised from the dead (Acts 2:29–32).

Jesus' death, burial, and resurrection comprise the Good News by which we are saved when we trust in Him (1 Cor. 15:1–4; Jn. 3:16; Rom. 10:1–13). However, this Good News is more than salvation in the here and now and more than a home in the heavenly sphere when we die. Those who trust in Jesus to take away their sins—the work of His First Coming—will get to enter into His earthly Kingdom when He establishes it—the work of His Second Coming.

Make no mistake. The glorious Kingdom anticipated in the first century is on its way when Jesus appears a second time. Are you ready for it?

CHAPTER SEVEN

God's Kingdom in the Sermon on the Mount

Chris Katulka

Prior to boarding the ship *Arbella* for the Massachusetts Bay Colony in 1630, Puritan John Winthrop preached a sermon to the ambitious colonists embarking on a life-threatening journey. Those brave men and women were setting sail to be part of a new community, which Winthrop called "a city upon a hill" that's watched by the world. Winthrop's message reverberated through American history and found meaning centuries later when President John F. Kennedy and President Ronald Reagan proclaimed America to be "a city upon a hill—the eyes of all people are upon us."

The Puritan preacher's message was inspiring; with only five words it gave vision and purpose. He believed this new community would be set apart to accomplish greater things purposed by God.

Even though Presidents Kennedy and Reagan properly attributed that quote to Winthrop, he didn't formulate it. Winthrop borrowed it from another sermon Jesus gave in one of the most popular portions of the Bible, the Sermon on the Mount, which is the first of Jesus' five discourses in the book of Matthew.

When Jesus taught the Sermon on the Mount, He was speaking to a Jewish audience waiting for God to change Israel's position in the world. Many who sat next to Jesus were probably waiting to hear the part of the story where God would free Israel from the oppressive Roman Empire and usher in an age of Messianic blessing. But Jesus never got to that part of the story.

He was more concerned with the spiritual condition of His disciples when He was offering them the long-awaited Kingdom. The Pharisees and scribes, who were Israel's spiritual role models, projected a corrupt form of righteousness. In Matthew 5—7, Jesus unraveled the religious leaders' hypocritical lifestyle to reveal the true righteousness of God's Law, Kingdom righteousness that comes from the inside out.

SETTING OF THE SERMON

The Kingdom of God was the centerpiece of Jewish belief and practice in the days of Jesus. Various sects of Judaism anticipated its restoration on Earth when the Messiah would come to rescue Israel, usher in God's Kingdom, and reign from Jerusalem. The Old Testament prophets promised this unique Kingdom's restoration: "To you [Judah] shall it come, even the former dominion shall come, the kingdom of the daughter of Jerusalem" (Mic. 4:8). Micah divinely predicted the restoration of the Kingdom similar to the way it was under King David, but even better. Jesus, the Son of David, began His ministry to Israel with Kingdom restoration in mind when He pronounced, "Repent, for the kingdom of heaven is at hand" (Mt. 4:17). The long-awaited Kingdom Old Testament prophets promised was knocking on Israel's door. Just prior to the Sermon on the Mount, Matthew recorded, "And Jesus went about all Galilee, teaching in their synagogues, preaching the gospel of the kingdom, and healing all kinds of sickness and all kinds of disease among the people" (4:23).

The crowds naturally were attracted to Jesus' words. After all, He was announcing the coming of the Kingdom. And He taught them with authority, which means He didn't rely on the layers of rabbinical teachings from the past to interpret the Scriptures. Instead, His teachings were direct revelation from God, similar to an Old Testament prophet who served as a mouthpiece of God's revelation. However, Jesus was not a mouthpiece for God. He is God. When the disciples heard Jesus teach, they heard directly from God's mouth.

Matthew spotlighted Jesus' divinity when he mentioned Jesus was healing people with various illnesses and diseases. Those healing actions served as signs, confirming that the Good News Jesus preached concerning the Kingdom was reliable and true. Matthew wanted His readers to know that the One who was about to teach the Sermon on the Mount was more than an itinerant rabbi visiting synagogues in the Galilee region. He's the Messiah Himself!

The Sermon on the Mount from Matthew opens with this setting: "And seeing the multitudes, He went up on a mountain, and when He was seated His disciples came to Him" (Mt. 5:1). The image of Jesus ascending a mountain is reminiscent of the mountain Moses ascended to receive the Torah (Law) from God (Ex. 19:20).[1]

The mountain motif in Exodus and Matthew represents God's way of communicating revelation about Himself and the way He expects His people to live within the coming Kingdom. Moses ascended Mount Sinai to receive the Law that would govern the tribes of Israel. Jesus ascended the mountainside to share with His disciples God's revelation concerning the heart of the Law, not the rabbis' interpretations. This is one of many similarities Jesus shared with Moses throughout the book of Matthew, as He was portrayed as the new Moses, the new Lawgiver.

Then Jesus opened His mouth and begin to teach. This was first time recorded in Matthew that the Son of God proclaimed to Israel how a citizen of God's Kingdom should look, sound, and act.[2]

CONTENT OF THE SERMON: THE BEATITUDES

The Sermon on the Mount began with eight beatitudes. Beatitudes are a form of wisdom literature that can be found in Psalms, Proverbs, and Ecclesiastes. But when Jesus preached them, He coupled godly wisdom with a prophetic reward received in God's Kingdom. The word *beatitude* comes from the Latin word *beati*, which means "blessed" or "happy." Jesus' audience would have been familiar with beatitudes from the Old Testament. The book of Psalms begins with one: "Blessed is the man who walks not in the counsel of the ungodly, nor stands in the path of sinners, nor sits in the seat of the scornful; but his delight is in the law of the Lord, and in His law he meditates day and night" (Ps. 1:1–2).

Jesus positioned the Beatitudes toward the front of His teaching to emphasize the spiritual characteristics a disciple should have in light of becoming a future Kingdom citizen.[3] Here are a few:

"Blessed are those who mourn, for they shall be comforted" (Mt. 5:4). The words in this statement are in juxtaposition. How can those who mourn be happy or blessed? The coexistence between happiness and mourning is found in the prophetic nature of the Sermon on the Mount.

Jesus echoed Isaiah 61:2–3 in this beatitude: "To proclaim the acceptable year of the LORD,...to comfort all who mourn, to console those who mourn in Zion." Isaiah prophesied the day God's restored Kingdom becomes a comforting reality to those who mourn.

"Blessed are the meek, for they will inherit the earth" (Mt. 5:5). Again a juxtaposition is found with the words in this verse. The meek and gentle are never depicted as those who inherit the earth. It's the powerful and greedy who accumulate wealth that come to own everything. Jesus taught that in God's Kingdom people who maintain a spiritual position of meekness will one day partake in His earthly reign.

Theology professor Michael Vlach argued that "the earth" refers to the land of Israel. Jesus quoted from Psalm 37:11, "But the meek shall inherit the earth, and shall delight themselves in the abundance of peace." Psalm 37 is about Israel and the Land. The audience listening to Jesus would have been expecting the Messiah to restore all of Israel to the Land. Simultaneously, the promise for Israel became a promise for all nations, when the King of kings will rule every nation, tribe, and tongue from Jerusalem.[4] Israel's blessing becomes the world's blessing.

"Blessed are those who hunger and thirst for righteousness, for they shall be filled" (Mt. 5:6). The longing in any disciple's heart, soul, and mind is for righteousness. Righteousness is the act of morally and ethically pleasing God by living out what His righteous commands demand of us. Followers of Jesus search for righteousness around them, but they continually come up empty. The world, in its current condition, is a righteousness desert, leaving disciples thirsty and hungry.

The prophetic nature of this beatitude shows that in God's coming Kingdom every disciple will be satisfied and filled. The Greek word for *filled* is also used to describe fattening animals.[5] There will be a day when righteousness will reign in God's Kingdom.

Jesus never said being a disciple was easy. We're called to be "poor in spirit" (v. 3) and "mourn" in this life (v. 4). We are called to be "meek" (v. 5) and gentle people, who "thirst for righteousness" (v. 6). We are called to be "merciful" (v. 7), "pure in heart" (v. 8), and "peacemakers" (v. 9) who will face persecution "for righteousness' sake" (v. 10).

Disciples' lives are marked by the tension of the here and now and the hope of God's Kingdom where we find our reward. When Jesus' disciples follow Him and live by these spiritual truths, they become "the salt of the earth" (v. 13) and "the light of the world" (v. 14). What sets us apart is the righteousness we long for that becomes the theme of the Sermon on the Mount.

THEME OF THE SERMON: RIGHTEOUSNESS FROM THE HEART

At the heart of the Sermon on the Mount is Isaiah's theme of righteousness. Righteousness will be the marker of the Messiah's reign, and it will be what characterizes the citizens of God's Kingdom.

When Isaiah described the coming of the Messiah and His Kingdom, he wrote, "Righteousness shall be the belt of His loins, and faithfulness the belt of His waist" (Isa. 11:5). Isaiah's imagery of righteousness and faithfulness is depicted as a belt wrapped around a waist. A belt is one of the most functional additions to a person's wardrobe because it holds up clothes. Righteousness and faithfulness will be the foundation that sustains and holds up the Messiah's Kingdom.

Righteousness in the Bible often refers to an ethical and moral standard. It's the upright, honorable, and virtuous approach to life. Isaiah's description of righteousness in God's Kingdom is directed at the moral and ethical rule of the Messiah. Unlike kings and leaders of the past and politicians of today, who are prone to corruption and the abuse of their citizens, Messiah's righteous rule will live up to the standards of God's Law that looks after and cares for everyone with divine justice. Psalm 72, a Messianic Psalm, begins, "Give the king Your judgments, O God, and Your righteousness to the king's Son. He will judge Your people with righteousness, and Your poor with justice" (vv. 1–2).

Jesus then began to expound on the Law. He first removed any doubt that His instruction and teaching was built on anything but the Law and the prophets. The religious leaders believed Jesus was teaching a righteousness that goes against what the Law of God demanded (Mt. 12:1–8; 15:1–20).[6] He did not come to upend God's Law or to overturn the Old Testament. Instead, He came to fulfill it: "Do not think that I came to destroy the Law or the Prophets. I did not come to destroy but to fulfill" (5:17).

The Law details God's righteous standards while revealing His nature and character. When Jesus emphatically detailed that He had not come to destroy the Law and prophets, He was signaling to His disciples that God's righteous standards found in the Old Testament will not be shaken and God's character will be manifest in His life. The

Law will remain the bedrock of God's Kingdom on Earth.

Jesus was more concerned with the corrupt form of "righteousness" the religious leaders displayed to His disciples. One thing is clear in Jesus' ministry: He was less focused on judging Israel's enemies, like Rome, and more focused on judging Israel's spiritual leaders who had abused their power in the way they shepherded God's people. Israel's spiritual relationship with God often determined how God managed Israel's relationship with their enemies. Jesus' attention was first on the spiritual well-being of His people, then judgment on the nations that exploited Israel.

The unrighteous hypocrisy of the Pharisees was held up against the righteousness of God's Law when Jesus gave the Sermon on the Mount. The Messiah condemned the Pharisees for publicly proclaiming their good deeds for everyone to see (6:2), praying loud enough for everyone to hear (v. 5), glorifying themselves when they fasted (v. 16), and judging others when they themselves had deep-seated sin in their lives (7:1–5).

The Pharisees and scribes, who were the spiritual shepherds of Israel, projected a false "righteousness" to the Jewish people. In Matthew 5:20, Jesus set the standard for entering into the coming Kingdom: "Unless your righteousness exceeds the righteousness of the scribes and Pharisees," you have no place in it. The righteousness God demands is not the righteousness the religious leaders lived from the outside, while corrupt on the inside. The righteousness Jesus taught His disciples is a righteousness that streams from the heart; it's obedience to God that comes from the inside out.

To illustrate true righteousness, Jesus compared it with the teachings of the Law: "You have heard that it was said to those of old." This was His way of saying the original recipients of the Mosaic Law heard these commands: "You shall not murder." "You shall not commit adultery." "Whoever divorces his wife, let him give her a certificate of divorce." "You shall not swear falsely." "An eye for an eye and a tooth for a tooth." "You shall love your neighbor and hate your enemy" (vv. 21, 27, 31, 33, 38, 43). However, Jesus, with the Kingdom of God in mind, took these laws written on tablets and conferred them to the disciple's heart.

For instance, as a Law-abiding Jewish person, you may never have committed murder. But Jesus said whoever is angry with his brother and insults his brother or calls him a fool has already broken the Law (vv. 21–23). As a law-abiding Jewish person, you may never have committed adultery, but Jesus said looking at a woman lustfully is the same as committing adultery in the heart (vv. 27–30). As a law-abiding Jewish person, you may never have sworn falsely in court; but if you've made a voluntary vow in God's name and broken it, it's the same as falsely testifying (vv. 33–37).

As a law-abiding Jewish person, you may believe in the philosophy of personal vengeance for wrongdoing—"an eye for an eye and a tooth for a tooth." But Jesus teaches you to practice pity, "turn the other cheek," and leave vengeance to God (vv. 38–42). As a law-abiding Jewish person, you may have loved your neighbor according to the Law but hated your enemy. Jesus said your enemy is your neighbor, too, and you should "bless those who curse you" (vv. 43–48).

If God's righteousness is the key to entering the coming Kingdom, then it's a righteousness that's characterized internally when the Law is placed in one's heart. The prophet Jeremiah predicted that one day a New Covenant would govern Israel and Judah. He wrote that it won't be like the covenant made at Sinai, where the Law was engraved on tablets. Instead, the New Covenant will be one in which God's Laws are written internally on minds and hearts (Jer. 31:31–33). Jesus taught that those laws engraved on tablets find their fuller meaning when they are written on a person's mind and heart.

God's righteous laws are the moral and ethical code disciples live by in light of God's coming Kingdom, but they are not what make you righteous. Righteousness is not gained by the Law; righteousness is imputed to those with faith in the Lawgiver. Genesis 15:6 says, "And he [Abram] believed in the LORD, and He accounted it to him for righteousness." It was Abram's trust and belief in God and His plan that made him righteous.

Disciples are deemed righteous in God's eyes when they place their faith in Jesus alone. Followers of Jesus have the Holy Spirit of God dwelling in them, another promise of the New Covenant (Ezek. 36:26). The apostle Paul wrote that when the Holy Spirit of God is working in the life of a believer, "what the law could not do in that it was weak through the flesh, God did by sending His own Son in the likeness of sinful flesh, on account of sin: He condemned sin in the flesh, that the righteous requirement of the law might be fulfilled in us who do not walk according to the flesh but according to the Spirit" (Rom. 8:3–4).

PURPOSE OF THE SERMON IN THE CHURCH

Jesus taught the Sermon on the Mount to show His disciples God's righteous standards for a Kingdom citizen. The problem is that God's earthly Kingdom was never realized in the Gospels. It was rejected when the spiritual leadership of Israel denied the Messiah and His offer for the Kingdom to come.

Since the Sermon on the Mount was connected to Jesus' offer of the Kingdom, how do His words fit in with the church today? In the same way that God's Kingdom has been postponed, has Jesus' teaching from the Sermon on the Mount been postponed as well? Or does this significant portion of Scripture have application for Christians today?

Some early dispensational scholars proposed the Sermon on the Mount is a constitution for Jewish people in the Millennial Kingdom and has little to no application for the church today.[7]

But when you read through the sermon, you hear Jesus encouraging His disciples to live righteous lives in light of the coming Kingdom. He even taught us to pray for forgiveness, for the ability to forgive others, and for refrain from temptation, all the while remaining vigilant to pray for His Kingdom to come. Jesus said His disciples will face persecution, are to be salt and light, should store up treasures in heaven, and shouldn't worry.

If the Sermon on the Mount is solely a constitution for the coming Kingdom and has no application for the life of a believer today, when we arrive in the Kingdom we will still face persecution and trials, we'll still need to be light in a dark place, and we'll still worry about mundane issues in life.

But this sermon shows future citizens of the Kingdom that God's Law remains the righteous standard for future Kingdom living. It is good and holy. The Law also finds its fulfillment when it's written on the heart of a disciple who lives out the Law from the inside out today.

Yes! The Sermon on the Mount will find its completion and fulfillment in the future earthly Kingdom established at Jesus Christ's Second Coming. However, disciples in the church today, who have the indwelling of the Holy Spirit, should look to this sermon as their righteous ethic that offers encouragement, hope, comfort, and instructions on how to walk as one of His disciples with hope that He's coming back again.

CONCLUSION

The Sermon on the Mount is one of the most popular sections of the Bible. If Jesus had a Twitter feed, His most retweeted, 140-character messages would come right from Matthew 5—7. Whether you're a Christian or not, you probably recognize these commands: "You are the salt of the earth." "You are the light of the world." "But whoever slaps you on your right cheek, turn the other to him also." "Love your enemies." "Do not let your left hand know what your right hand is doing." "In this manner, therefore, pray: Our Father in heaven, hallowed be Your name."

Many people cherry-pick these teachings without looking into the Kingdom context that surrounds the Sermon on the Mount. Jesus didn't simply want to leave us with some spiritual one-liners. He was laying the foundation for how a Kingdom citizen should look, sound, and act both today and later in God's restored Kingdom on Earth.

CHAPTER EIGHT

God's Kingdom Offered to Israel

Bruce Scott

On the top of an imposing mountain in modern-day Jordan, just east of the Dead Sea, are the ruins of ancient Machaerus. Around 90 BC, Alexander Jannaeus, the Hasmonean king of Judea, built a fortress there.[1] Later, Herod the King, as was his penchant, upgraded its fortifications and added a luxurious palace, and it had its own prison.

According to Josephus, one of Herod's sons, Herod Antipas, imprisoned John the Baptist there.[2] John's crime was preaching against the illicit marriage Antipas had with Herodias, his brother Philip's wife (Mk. 6:17–18).

In his earlier ministry, John announced that One was coming who "will thoroughly clean out His threshing floor, and gather His wheat into the barn" (Mt. 3:12). John's harvest analogy was meant to emphasize the nearness of the promised Messiah and His Kingdom. This is why both John and Jesus' initial message to the people was, "Repent, for the kingdom of heaven is at hand!" (3:2; 4:17).

But sitting alone in the dark and dank prison of Machaerus, John the Baptist, perhaps out of discouragement or depression, apparently began to have a twinge of doubt. He had heard about the miraculous works of Christ. But so far there was no accompanying Kingdom with those works. So John, like the apostle Paul later on, needed confirmation regarding the ministry message he preached about Jesus. He needed to know that he had not "run, in vain" (Gal. 2:2).

For this reason, John sent his disciples to ask Jesus the primary question every searching soul must ask: "Are You the Coming One, or do we look for another?" In reply, Jesus said, "Go and tell John the things which you hear and see" (Mt. 11:3–4). Why did Jesus respond to John in this way? Why did He not respond with a simple, "Yes, I am the Coming One"?

It is one thing to claim to be the Messiah; it's another to authenticate that claim with biblically predicted, verifiable, miraculous works. Throughout history, only one person has ever done that: Jesus Christ.

Nevertheless, Matthew recorded, particularly in chapters 8—12, that even though the King and His Kingdom were proclaimed, they were also persecuted. And the consequences that followed were devastating for the nation of Israel, namely, the King and His Kingdom were postponed.

THE KING AND KINGDOM PROCLAIMED

Matthew 9:35 summarizes Jesus' early ministry well: "Then Jesus went about all the cities and villages, teaching in their synagogues, preaching the gospel of the kingdom, and healing every sickness and every disease among the people." In chapters 8—12, Matthew recorded numerous occasions where Jesus performed astounding miracles attesting to His Messianic credentials and the imminency of the Kingdom.

For example, coming down from the mountain after giving His sermon (chaps. 5—7), Jesus first encountered an outcast from society, a man afflicted with leprosy (8:2-4). Although most people would run from the leper, Jesus touched him and healed him instantaneously and completely.

Going on to His headquarters in Capernaum, a godly Gentile who was a Roman centurion, entreated Jesus to heal his paralyzed servant who was suffering great pain (vv. 5–13). Jesus offered to go to the servant to heal him. But the centurion, demonstrating his great faith, requested that Jesus only speak a word and his servant would be healed. Jesus did so, "and his servant was healed that same hour."

Jesus then healed the apostle Peter's mother-in-law of a fever. Later that evening, Jesus healed other people, some who were demon-possessed and some who had other afflictions (vv. 14–17). Matthew declared that Jesus' miraculous healings fulfilled the Messianic prophecy in Isaiah 53:4, "He Himself took our infirmities and bore our sicknesses."

As Jesus and His disciples were getting into a boat to go to the other side of the Sea of Galilee, a scribe approached Jesus, called Him

GOD'S KINGDOM OFFERED TO ISRAEL

Teacher, and asserted he would follow Jesus wherever He went. Jesus responded by referring to Himself as the Son of Man, a Messianic title in the same vein as Son of David (Mt. 8:18–20).

Later on, while Jesus was sleeping, a great storm whipped up the sea and threatened to swamp the boat in which Jesus and His disciples were sailing. Panicked, the disciples woke Jesus up and begged Him to save them. Jesus rebuked the winds and the sea, and all became perfectly calm (vv. 23–27).

Upon landing, two violent, demon-possessed men confronted Jesus. The demons within the men, although fallen, unholy angels, still acknowledged Jesus for who He truly was: "Son of God." Jesus cast out the demons and sent them into a nearby herd of swine, which subsequently drowned in the sea (vv. 28–32).

Jesus then went back to Capernaum. While there, He healed a paralytic. He used the occasion once again to refer to Himself with the Messianic title Son of Man and to affirm His authority to forgive sins (9:1–8).

From there, Jesus accompanied a synagogue official whose daughter just died. While on the way, a woman who suffered a hemorrhage for twelve years touched the hem of Jesus' garment. At that very hour, she was healed. Jesus went on to the official's home where He took the dead girl by the hand, and she came back to life (vv. 18–26).

Going on, two blind men followed Jesus, crying out for His mercy while acclaiming Him as the "Son of David," the standard title Jewish people used when referring to the Messiah. Jesus granted their request, touched their eyes, and gave them their sight (vv. 27–31).

Following that healing, Jesus cast out a demon from a mute man. Afterward, the man spoke; and the multitudes marveled at the miracle (vv. 32–33).

Seeing the needy multitudes as sheep without a shepherd, Jesus multiplied His ministry by sending out twelve disciples. In doing so, He gave them authority "over unclean spirits, to cast them out, and to heal all kinds of sickness and all kinds of disease" and even to raise the dead (10:1, 8). Their commission was not to go to Gentiles or Samaritans but only to "the lost sheep of the house of Israel" (v. 6). Jesus also gave them a specific message: "And as you go, preach, saying, 'The kingdom of heaven is at hand'" (v. 7). And once again, as He gave His disciples their instructions, Jesus referred to Himself with the Messianic title "Son of Man" (v. 23).

Sometime later, on a Sabbath day in a synagogue, a man with a withered hand was brought before Jesus. Jesus told the man to stretch out his hand. When he did so, his hand was restored to normal (12:9–13). Many continued to follow Jesus, and He healed them all (v. 15).

Finally, the climactic example of Jesus' Messianic power came in verses 22–23. A demon-possessed man, who also was blind and mute, was brought to Jesus. As expected, Jesus freed the man from demonic possession and healed him completely. This particular demonstration of Jesus' power is climactic because of the response of those around Him and the repercussions of it.

What was the response from the crowds? "And all the multitudes were amazed and said, 'Could this be the Son of David?'" (v. 23). The people who witnessed Jesus healing the blind and mute man were pondering whether or not He could actually be the long-awaited Messiah, based on what they had just seen. But the Pharisees, who also were present, repudiated such a conclusion.

Through these examples, Matthew demonstrated Jesus had power over the elements of creation (such as the wind and the sea), disease (even from a distance), fevers, paralysis, long-term illnesses (such as hemorrhaging), blindness, muteness, disabilities (such as a withered hand), demon possession, and even death itself. But Jesus did not perform His miracles haphazardly or to entertain. He did them all with a purpose in mind: to substantiate the message He proclaimed. This is why Jesus said to report to John "the things which you *hear* and *see*" (11:4, emphasis added).

Jesus claimed to be the Messiah. He referred to Himself as such. He did not correct others who called Him with that title. Additionally, He proclaimed the imminency of the Kingdom and demonstrated the supernatural qualities of the Kingdom with His miraculous deeds and acts of healing. What more, then, would be needed to convince Israel that Jesus was the promised Messiah and the Kingdom was now at hand?

John wrote in his Gospel that not all of Jesus' deeds and miraculous signs were recorded in New Testament Scripture. If they had been, John speculated that "even the world itself could not contain the books that would be written" (Jn. 21:25). But the ones that were recorded are sufficient for someone to "believe that Jesus is the Christ, the Son of God" (20:31).

Therefore, despite the somewhat limited number of recorded, authenticating deeds, one cannot honestly assert there is insufficient proof that Jesus is the promised Messiah. It is not a matter of insufficient proof. It is a matter of unwillingness to believe the proof.

THE KING AND KINGDOM PERSECUTED

An unwillingness to believe was the condition of the religious leaders of Jesus' day. They, who represented the nation, are seen throughout the Gospels as regularly and consistently pushing back against Jesus and His message of the Kingdom. Even though they had an adequate amount of evidence in both word and deed (3:2), they still challenged and opposed Jesus' right to the throne of David. In Matthew 8—12, we see ever-intensifying examples of that resistance.

In Matthew 9:2–3, we find the first recorded instance of official opposition against Jesus. When He said to the paralytic, "Your sins are forgiven you," some of the scribes said to themselves, "This Man blasphemes!" Blasphemy is attributing to God something that is untrue or attributing to oneself something that should be attributed to God. Here, in the eyes of the scribes, Jesus attributed to Himself the authority to forgive sins, which only God has the right to do.

Later, the Pharisees condemned Jesus for eating "with tax collectors and sinners" (v. 11). By associating with sinners, Jesus had, in the minds of the self–righteous and hypocritical Pharisees, defiled Himself, thus becoming disqualified from being the righteous Branch of David (Jer. 23:5).

When Jesus cast out a demon, healing the man who was mute (Mt. 9:33), the people "marveled, saying, 'It was never seen like this in Israel!'" The Pharisees, jealous and protective of their popularity (e.g., Mt. 27:18), tried to dampen the enthusiasm of the people toward Jesus: "The Pharisees said, 'He casts out demons by the ruler of the demons'" (9:34). Later we read that the ruler of the demons to whom the Pharisees referred was called Beelzebub (10:25; 12:24), the chief prince, or ruler, of the demons, which, of course, would be the devil or Satan.[3] This appalling accusation reached its pinnacle in chapter 12.

But first, Jesus' disciples and later Jesus as well, were falsely accused of breaking God's Law against working on the Sabbath. As for the disciples, they plucked heads of grain from the fields and ate them. "When the Pharisees saw it, they said to Him, 'Look, Your disciples are doing what is not lawful to do on the Sabbath!'" (12:2). When in the synagogue on the same Sabbath, the religious leaders tried to entrap Jesus by bringing forward a man with a withered hand and asking Him, "Is it lawful to heal on the Sabbath?" (v. 10). Jesus corrected the Pharisees' understanding of the Sabbath by pointing out that He was "Lord even of the Sabbath" (v. 8) and "it is lawful to do good on the Sabbath" (v. 12).

The Pharisees' response was shocking and revealed both their hearts' condition and receptivity to Jesus' proclamation of His Messiahship and impending Kingdom. "Then the Pharisees went out and plotted against Him, how they might destroy Him" (v. 14). This is the first mention of the religious leaders plotting together for the express purpose of destroying, or killing, Jesus.

Note the paradox here. These men were supposed to be the spiritual leaders of the people and caretakers of God's Word. Instead, we find them plotting together to murder the promised Messiah, God's Anointed One, in direct contradiction to the very Word of God they were supposed to promote and protect.

And then, once again, when Jesus cast out the blind and mute man's demon and the multitudes were wondering if Jesus might be the Messiah, the Pharisees thought it was necessary to discount what had just happened. "Now when the Pharisees heard it they said, 'This fellow does not cast out demons except by Beelzebub, the ruler of the demons'" (v. 24). This was the same outrageous charge the Pharisees threw at Jesus earlier (9:34). Only here, Matthew recorded Jesus' reaction to it; and it was not a good one for the Pharisees.

The final expression of resistance to Jesus and His Kingdom found in these chapters is in Matthew 12:38, "Then some of the scribes and Pharisees answered, saying, 'Teacher, we want to see a sign from You.'" A sign was an attesting miracle. They wanted proof. But Jesus had already given them plenty of proof. They were not asking because they did not have sufficient data. They were asking because it was their way of demeaning Jesus and exercising authority over Him. They did not realize that in asking for proof, they were displaying the evil intent of their hearts and lack of trust in Jesus' words.

Matthew's examples of opposition are put forth only to demonstrate the truth of John 1:11, "He came to His own, and His own did not receive Him." The ultimate example, of course, was when the chief priests answered Pilate, "We have no king but Caesar!" (19:15). And Jesus was subsequently crucified.

Jesus rightly observed earlier, "And from the days of John the Baptist until now the kingdom of heaven suffers violence, and the violent take it by force" (Mt. 11:12). The religious leaders of Jesus' day did not want the Kingdom Jesus was offering. They wanted their own version of it on their own terms (vv. 16–19). So they repulsed the Messiah's forerunner, John the Baptist (Mt. 21:32; Lk 7:30), and then handed the Messiah over to be violently killed.

But people cannot deny the Holy One, ask for a murderer (Barabbas) to be granted to them, and kill the Prince of life (Acts 3:14–15) without consequences.

THE KING AND KINGDOM POSTPONED

Jesus said, "For as the lightning that flashes out of one part under heaven shines to the other part under heaven, so also the Son of Man will be in His day. But first He must suffer many things and be *rejected by this generation*" (Lk. 17:24–25, emphasis mine).

The repercussions of that rejection are significant.

For Israel, the rejection of the Messiah had devastating effects. It was not that the Kingdom was redefined. Rather, the Kingdom was no longer "at hand." It was postponed. Instead, there would be an interregnum, which Dictionary.com defines as "any period during which a state has no ruler" (cf. Hos. 3:4–5). The King and His Kingdom went away until such time God brings Israel into a state of true repentance.

How do we know the Kingdom was postponed? Matthew 8—12 give us some indication, while other passages are more definitive. For example, when Jesus sent out His disciples to proclaim that the Kingdom of heaven was at hand, He also predicted there would be resistance to their ministry (10:16–23). In fact, He said they would suffer extreme persecution and "not have gone through the cities of Israel before the Son of Man comes" (v. 23). These things never happened to the disciples during Jesus' First Coming. Therefore, Jesus must have been addressing future Jewish witnesses living in another period of time, specifically during the Tribulation period, just before the Second Coming of the King and the actual establishment of His Kingdom. Thus, an interregnum is implied.

An interregnum is also implied by how Jesus reacted to the persecution He endured. In Matthew 11:16 and 12:41–42 (also 23:36), Jesus addressed His contemporaries as "this generation." By using this phrase, Jesus didn't embrace His generation. Rather, He separated Himself from the nation of Israel, thus implying the Kingdom was no longer imminent.

Jesus also rebuked certain cities for not repenting, even though they saw His mighty works (11:20–24). He condemned the Pharisees for committing the unpardonable sin, that is, attributing the power of the Holy Spirit within Jesus to the work of the devil (12:25–32). Jesus also declared that His adversaries would be judged for every careless word they spoke about Him (vv. 33–37).

Jesus then went to the core of the matter by condemning His "evil and adulterous generation" for not taking Him at His word (vv. 38–45). Instead, they wanted a sign. Jesus said there was going to be only one, major, all-time confirming, supernatural sign given to His generation: His resurrection from the dead. Jesus contrasted His own unrepentant generation with that of repentant Gentiles, such as the men of Nineveh and the Queen of Sheba. Those Gentiles repented when they heard the proclamation of God's Word. (Verse 41 is the last time the word *repent* is used in Matthew.) Jesus' generation did not. Even though Jesus came to His generation and did what was necessary to prove His credentials and offer the Kingdom, His generation rejected Him. Consequently, Israel's spiritual state was going to be worse than before. In fact, Paul wrote, "blindness in part has happened to Israel" (Rom. 11:25).

In the first part of Matthew's Gospel, Jesus proclaimed that the Kingdom was at hand. But after chapter 12, He began to speak in terms of the "mysteries of the kingdom" (13:11), building His church (16:18), sitting on His glorious throne (using the future tense, 19:28), and the Great Commission (28:18–20). All of these point to an interregnum.

In Luke 19:11, Luke made it clear that right before Jesus' triumphal entry into Jerusalem on Palm Sunday, the people thought the Kingdom was about to appear immediately. But it did not. And, thus, in the following verses, Jesus told a parable indicating there would be an interregnum.

Finally, in Matthew 21:43 Jesus specified that His generation would not experience the Kingdom. It was being taken away from them. Instead, a future generation of Israel, one that repents, will get to enter it.

Like the ancient Israelites who did not enter the Promised Land because of their unbelief, it is tragic that Jesus' generation did not enter the promised Kingdom for the same reason. Nevertheless, the apostle Paul wrote, "Through their [Israel's] fall, to provoke them to jealousy, salvation has come to the Gentiles" (Rom. 11:11). In other words, from a spiritual point of view that considers God's sovereignty in all things, God used Israel's moral choice to bring about a higher purpose: "The stone which the builders rejected has become the chief cornerstone" (Ps. 118: 22). Even though the "stone" was rejected, God brought something good out of it anyway, namely, salvation to the world.

THE KING AND OUR RESPONSE

"Are You the Coming One, or do we look for another?" John the Baptist asked (Mt. 11:3).

Today Jesus, in essence, responds, "I am the promised Messiah. Someday I will return in fulfillment of the Scriptures to bring in the theocratic Kingdom spoken of in the Law, the prophets, and the writings. In the meantime, read My Word. Read of My good deeds, My death for your sins, and My resurrection. Believe I did all this for you. And blessed is he who is not offended because of Me."

CHAPTER NINE

God's Parables of the Kingdom

Clarence Johnson

Stories capture readers' and listeners' attentions and draw them in to consider new ideas and new ways of living. They are effective means of teaching truth. More and more, writers and teachers are using stories as vehicles to convey the points they want to get across.

Jesus, too, knew the power of story. It's a method He used often in His teaching, even when talking about God's coming Kingdom.

CONTEXT OF THE DISCOURSE

Leading up to those parables, one can only imagine the disciples' apprehension and the Messiah's dismay caused by the Jewish leaders' vitriolic and murderous response to Jesus' Messianic miracles in Matthew 12. The Pharisees represented the Jewish nation, and their rejection of the divinely authenticated King and Kingdom received a potent and divine indictment against both them and their generation.

Jesus' censure in Matthew 11 and 12 indicates that the growing negativity toward Him and the proclaimed Kingdom were far more serious than the grumblings of a few pessimists or cynics. Their eyes and ears were closed to His Messianic claims; their hearts were hardened and impenetrable to the truth. The full intensity of their opposition would not be fully demonstrated until the week of the crucifixion.

Their response is a major turning point in Jesus' ministry and the future of the Jewish people. Why wouldn't they listen? What would happen to the promised Kingdom Jesus proclaimed to be at hand?

We need to understand the discourse in Matthew 13 within the larger context of emerging Jewish hostility and rejection of King and

Kingdom. Without such contextual restrictions, interpretation of the parables may be built on preconceived perspectives, the reader's theological leanings, or allegorical inspiration.

Alexander Bruce devoted a considerable amount of time pressing this point home in his systematic study of the passage: "A man's opinions are very apt to be influenced by the time in which he lives and the community to which he belongs, and his interpretation of any portion of Scripture that has been made to do service on either side is only too likely to exhibit manifest traces of the bias thence received."[1]

After the religious leaders publically accused Him of being empowered by Beelzebub, Jesus went away and sat by the sea. As a large crowd of people gathered around Him and pressed in, He moved from the shoreline and sat down in a boat on the water's edge. This action was not an attempt to escape but an opportunity to speak to the people in parables (Mt. 13:1–3). Many of the people congregating on the shore were undeniably there only to witness His miraculous power. Regardless of individual motives, to the compassionate eyes and heart of the One who came to seek and to save the lost, they were like sheep without a shepherd, weary and scattered.

CONTENT OF THE DISCOURSE

When Jesus spoke to the gathered crowd, he told parables. The term *parable* is a transliteration of the Greek compound παραβολή (*parabolē*) that literally means to throw alongside or set alongside in comparison. A parable places a well-known example or illustration from nature or life alongside an abstract spiritual or ethical truth for the purpose of expressing the comparative similarities or differences.

James Boice offered this definition:

> *A parable is a story from real life or a real-life situation from which a moral or spiritual truth is drawn.... In the parables of Jesus not every detail has a meaning. In fact, to try to force meaning into each of the details produces strange and sometimes even demonstrably false doctrines. Parables are merely real-life stories from which one or possibly a few basic truths can be drawn.*[2]

Although such definitions suffice within the scope of this chapter, they are not always adequate for an extensive study of each of the forty-five times the word *parable* appears in the Gospels. The Ryrie Study Bible makes note of how this word is used: "The Greek word for 'parable' is a broad term and may refer to a simile,...a metaphor,...a proverb,...a story,...an allegory,...etc.... Some are short sayings designed to inculcate a single truth. Others, like the sower (vv. 3–20), have detailed interpretation."[3]

Due to the complex nature of parables and their interpretations, Matthew 13 presents some formidable expository challenges. A double-edged sword of interpretation cuts across all theological perspectives:

While the tendency of expositors to allegorize parables was a mistake, some parables have more than one climax, and the stories are organisms, so that several points of comparison might arise (e.g., the sower and different soils). One must also avoid generalizing, for Jesus is not illustrating general truths but preaching the kingdom of God.[4]

Evidence of such misappropriation of allegory or generalization is easily recognized in the strikingly diverse contradictory teachings and writings of highly respected, godly teachers from various theological backgrounds.

DIVISION OF THE PARABLES

Matthew 13 records eight parables Jesus taught on that day. An obvious division in the text sorts them according to their public or private nature. He spoke four to the crowd on the shore of Galilee (vv. 1–3) and later shared four with the disciples once they had gathered privately in a nearby house, following the dismissal of the crowd (v. 36). Some scholars only recognize seven parables as part of the discourse: four to the multitudes and three to the disciples, concluding with the parable of the dragnet.

The preferred division recognizes the public and private distinction but also partitions the parables thematically. The parable of the sower is introductory and, therefore, stands alone as foundational to understanding the others (Mk. 4:13). The wheat and the tares, mustard seed, and leaven reveal different oppositions to God's Kingdom. The treasure and pearl assert the preciousness of the Kingdom, and the dragnet declares the adjudication of the Kingdom. Lastly, the parable of the householder, like that of the sower, stands alone in summary, presenting the new responsibilities of the disciples in relation to the new parabolic revelation.

Seeing the first and last parables as the opening and closing to the discourse is textually justified. They both omit being introduced by "the Kingdom of heaven is like." Yet, each of the other six parables are so identified (Mt. 13: 24, 31, 33, 44, 45, 47). Notice that the parable of the householder does contain this phrase in verse 52. However, "the kingdom of heaven" is not the grammatical subject of the parabolic comparison. The comparison is in the scribe who "is like a householder." The phrase "instructed concerning the kingdom of heaven" modifies "every scribe."

As recorded in Mark, Jesus obviously shared the purpose and content of the parables and the explanation of the parable of the sower during His later, private session with the disciples. Matthew, however, places them in juxtaposition with the first parable for literary effect, further emphasizing its foundational importance. Even though only two explanations are included in Matthew's Gospel, most likely Jesus enlightened the disciples on other parables as well: "When they were alone, He explained all things to His disciples" (Mk. 4:34).

PURPOSE OF THE PARABLES

Following Jesus' lessons to the crowd, the disciples, noticing the change in Jesus' methodology, asked, "Why do you speak to them in parables?" His answer is twofold: (1) to reveal truth and (2) to conceal truth (Mt.13:10–17). By grace, on the basis of their faith, the disciples were endowed with the ability to comprehend the truth contained in the parables. They were truly blessed because what was being made manifest for the first time was something many prophets and righteous men before them desired to see, but it was not the time for it to be unveiled (vv. 16–17). To all who truly accept the Messiah, the truth would be revealed.

To those whose hearts were hardened in unbelief and rejection of the King and Kingdom, the parables made no sense. Jesus said, "I speak to them in parables, because seeing they do not see, and hearing they do not hear, nor do they understand" (v. 13). His use of Isaiah 6:9–10 links His current rejection to Israel's hardened heart during Isaiah's day, which brought a judgment of spiritual blindness and deafness. However difficult it is to grasp that God would withhold truth from some people while revealing it to others, this action may also be seen as an act of grace, as Stanley Toussaint explained:

> *By so concealing the truth the King is following His own injunction not to give that which is holy to dogs nor to cast pearls before swine (Matthew 7:6). In veiling the truth from those with hardened hearts the Lord was actually exercising grace. For, as Plummer says, "They were saved from the guilt of rejecting the truth, for they were not allowed to recognize it."*[5]

TRUTHS IN THE PARABLES

Jesus identified the truth contained in the parables as "the mysteries of the Kingdom of heaven" (13:11). The English word *mystery* is transliterated from the Greek μυστήριον (*mystērion*). In Colossians 1:26, Paul defined a mystery as that "which has been hidden from ages and from generations, but now has been revealed to His saints." A mystery is something that was not made known to people in other ages but now was divinely revealed (Rom. 16:25–26; Eph. 3:5–6).

Toussaint continued,

> *Since the Lord refers to these parables as containing truths which are mysteries, one may infer that they contain facts which were not revealed before the time He spoke them. That this is the significance of* μυστήριον *[mystērion] in Matthew 13 is verified by verses seventeen and thirty-five.*[6]

Jesus, by way of the parables, was divinely revealing truth about the Kingdom of heaven that was not revealed in the Old Testament or His earlier ministry. But He now disclosed it in response to the people rejecting Him as Messiah.

The mysteries belong to the "kingdom of heaven," the sphere of the mysteries. This is the same Kingdom John, Jesus, and the disciples proclaimed (Mt. 3:2; 4:17; 10:7). It is a literal, earthly Kingdom; it is Jewish; it was prophesied in the Old Testament and confirmed by Jesus and the apostles. "Unless one is born again, he cannot see the kingdom of God" (Jn. 3:3).

Despite claims regarding dissimilarities between the Kingdom of heaven and the Kingdom of God, they are synonymous. The confusing original and updated Scofield notes on Matthew 6:33 create various interpretive contradictions and complications. For a more complete examination of this issue, see chapter 6, "Kingdom Anticipation in the First Century."

Many interpretations of the "kingdom of heaven" in Matthew 13 redefine or rename it the "mystery Kingdom" or "mystery form of the Kingdom." Needless to say, Jesus did not announce a new or corrected meaning for the Kingdom of heaven He and His disciples proclaimed. Nor did He change His offer to a different Kingdom in a "mystery" form. To the Jew, there were two ages: the age of waiting for the Messiah and the Messianic Kingdom Age. The Old Testament did not contain prophetic truth regarding a time between the advent of the suffering Servant and His Second Advent as conquering King.

The prophets saw one advent at which time both redemption and judgment would come. Israel's enemies would be defeated, spiritual hearts would be changed, and the Messiah would rule and reign from Jerusalem. The newly disclosed mysteries contain additional truth about the timetable of the Kingdom prophesied for the Jews. The parables of the Kingdom of heaven reveal a period of postponement, beginning with the rejection of the Messiah and concluding with the establishment of the Millennial Kingdom when Christ returns to rule in glory and power.

Toussaint's commentary adds illumination to this issue:

> *Because of the Jewish rejection of the Messiah, the promised kingdom is now held in abeyance. The parables of Matthew 13 reveal new truths involving the preparation for the establishment of the kingdom during this time of postponement which was not predicted in Daniel's seventy weeks or other Old Testament prophecies.*[7]

This interadvent time is not the Church Age, but it does include the epoch when the church is on Earth. It also includes the latter part of Jesus' earthly ministry up to the church's beginning at Pentecost and the 70th week of Daniel that follows the church's Rapture.

EXPLANATION OF THE DISCOURSE

PARABLE OF THE SOWER (MATTHEW 13:3–9, 18–23)

The introductory parable of the sower is not likened to the Kingdom of heaven and thus reveals no mystery. The interpretation of this public parable is straightforward as it is given in Jesus' private explanation to His disciples. The act of sowing seed, the types of ground mentioned, and the potential results were all familiar to the crowd.

The seed symbolizes God's broadcast Word of the Kingdom, and the four soils represent hearers' different heart attitudes and receptions to the Word. Some have hardened hearts like the trodden wayside or pathway. The Word never pierces the surface and is easily snatched away by the devil's schemes before it has any impact. Other people are quickly excited by the word but accept it superficially. With no penetration, it easily withers and dies. The thorny ground is hearts filled with worldliness that takes priority and chokes out the Word, making it unfruitful. Good-soil people hear and understand the Word, taking it to themselves where it takes root, grows, and bears fruit of varying amounts.

People have received God's Word these ways in every age past, present, and future. The hearts of those listening to Jesus that day would also have different responses to the Word. Therefore, the admonition "He who has ears to hear, let him hear!" ends the parable.

Opposition to the message of the King and His Kingdom is great, but some people will believe and bear fruit. This truth forms a foundation for understanding the other parables. Expectations that the path to the Kingdom would be lined with open hearts and a widespread welcome to God's Word are false. It has not been that way since Adam's fall; throughout the days of the patriarchs, Moses, kings, and prophets; and Jesus' First Advent. Nor will it be so at His Second Coming and the associated great battles to launch the Kingdom.

PARABLE OF THE WHEAT AND THE TARES (MATTHEW 13:24–30, 36–43)

The parable of the wheat and tares began the unveiling of the mysteries about the age between the Messiah's two advents. Throughout this time, the Lord will be sowing the sons of the Kingdom throughout the world. In an act of aggression, the devil will disguise sons of the wicked one and covertly sow them alongside the righteous to oppose their fruitfulness and confuse the world. This coexistence will continue throughout the entire time between advents. Judgment will be delayed until the end of the age when the sons of the wicked one will be gathered, removed from the world, and eternally judged. At the same time, the sons of the Kingdom will be gathered into the Lord's barn, the Millennial Kingdom. Some people see this parable as the church filled with both saved and unsaved people. In refutation, D. A. Carson wrote,

> *Nowhere in Matthew does "kingdom"...become "church."... The parable does not address the church situation at all but explains how the kingdom can be present in the world while not yet wiping out all opposition. That must await the harvest. The parable deals with eschatological expectation, not ecclesiological deterioration.*[8]

PARABLES OF THE MUSTARD SEED AND LEAVEN (MATTHEW 13:31–33)

Countless interpretations of the parables of the mustard seed and leaven are profoundly contradictory. The main interpretive question is whether or not they symbolize the progressive influence of good or evil. Unlike the first two parables, Jesus' explanation, if shared with the disciples, is not recorded in the Bible.

The view that these parables represent the universal growth of the church and/or the gospel is untenable when viewed within the unity of the parables, the nature of the real-life elements, and corresponding scriptural teaching. Taking the parables as a unit, both are public and coincide with the theme of obstruction to Kingdom progress. We also must consider that biblical prophecy declares a progressive growth of unrestrained worldwide evil prior to the Kingdom's manifestation, rather than an unhindered expansion of good. Plus, Jesus' teaching always relates leaven with evil.

The life cycle of the mustard herb is brief. Starting with a tiny seed, it grows rapidly, sometimes to heights greater than ten feet. In a short time, it blossoms, goes to seed, and dies. As an annual, it is dependent on the dissemination of its seeds for proliferation. Unimpeded, what begins with one small seed can become pervasive, abundantly spreading its life through copious seeds.

Like the mustard plant spreading its seeds, the Kingdom message will be disseminated throughout the interadvent period. It would seem that insignificant seeds of truth might pervasively spread throughout the field of the entire world. However, similar to the parable of the sower, the forces of evil—like birds roosting in the midst—devour the seed before it is spread, hindering the dissemination and multiplication of the message.

Leaven, too, is pervasive. A small amount spreads its fermentation until stopped by heat or something else. Left alone, it eventually sours the entire host. The wheat flour represents the fruitfulness of those who properly receive the Word of the Kingdom. Yeast, representing evil, is mixed into a limited portion of the meal, souring all that it touches. During the Kingdom postponement, the fruitfulness of the sons of the Kingdom will be partially corrupted by the introduction of evil and false teaching.

PARABLES OF THE HIDDEN TREASURE AND PEARL OF GREAT PRICE (MATTHEW 13:44–46)

Jesus told the parables of the hidden treasure and pearl of great price only to His disciples. In contrast to the mixed crowd, He spoke to the disciples as those who had appropriately received the Word. The theme of His teaching then shifted from obstacles of the Kingdom to the precious value of the Kingdom.

The common understanding of these parables identifies the man and the merchant as Christ and the process of selling and buying as His sacrifice and death to purchase Israel, the treasure, and the church, the pearl. A closer look tells us the Lord did not stumble on Israel in the world by accident, nor did He search for the best pearl among other pearls before finding the church. He chose both before the foundation of the world. Finding a biblical bridge between the pearl and the church is at best indirect, especially since the church was yet to be revealed.

No one can ever purchase the Kingdom; entrance comes by grace through faith. Jesus called people to "seek first the kingdom of God and His righteousness" (6:33). He also taught that one must be willing to forsake all to follow Him. People who do so will be rewarded a hundredfold in the Kingdom (19:29). "These parables speak of the value of the kingdom and the intense desire that must accompany those who seek to enter it. One should value the kingdom above all else."[9]

In spite of the rejection, postponement, and obstacles, the Kingdom is not lost. Entrance to the Kingdom is still available, and it is precious beyond everything this world has to offer.

THE PARABLE OF THE DRAGNET (MATTHEW 13:47–50)

God commanded Israel to insulate itself from the world to maintain purity. The mysteries revealed that God's plan now placed His people in the world to coexist with those who oppose the King and Kingdom. The Old Testament promised the adjudication of the wicked at the Messiah's advent, but His rejection delayed that judgment until the return of the King to establish His Kingdom. Then, separating the wicked from the just will be like separating fish after a dragnet is drawn in to shore and good fish are kept and the bad thrown away. The angels will draw in the net and cast the wicked into eternal fire where there is wailing and gnashing of teeth. (See also Matthew 19:28 and 25:31.)

PARABLE OF THE HOUSEHOLDER (MATTHEW 13:52)

The final parable summarizes the disciples' responsibility now that they had been blessed with this new revelation. Rather than nullifying the old covenants and promises of the Kingdom, the newly revealed mysteries provided details about their timetable of fulfillment and the interadvent period's character. The disciples were then charged with dispensing one treasure of truth, the old and new together, to those who await the coming Kingdom.

SUMMARY

From God's perspective, there is no postponement or addition of an age. It is all part of His eternal, singular plan to bring about the promised Kingdom and restoration of all things. The interadvent period is not the Kingdom, the mystery Kingdom, or a mystery form of the Kingdom. It is not the church. God was not surprised by the people's rejection of Messiah, nor was the apparent postponement a reactive afterthought.

During this interadvent period, the golden cord of a restored Kingdom that weaves the promises of all ages together may appear distant and hidden. Yet, it is just below the surface, waiting to be revealed in resplendent grandeur when Christ returns. On the other hand, the crimson cord of redemption has wound its way from Genesis 3:15 through the cross to a glorious resurrection from the dark, proclaiming that the price has been paid and the restoration of all things is now possible.

So let's keep telling the story of God's redemption and living it out daily.

CHAPTER TEN

Ministry of the Rejected King

Tom Simcox

Rejection hurts, no matter what form it takes. A 10-year-old boy isn't chosen for a sports team. A high-schooler asks a girl to a party and is turned down. Parents throw a teenager out of the house with the admonition never to come back. A husband rejects his wife after twenty years and files for divorce. A woman with a stellar résumé is rejected for a job for which she is well-qualified.

Jesus, too, experienced the sting of rejection, which had far-reaching consequences.

After the Jewish religious and political leaders rejected Him, Jesus ceased offering the Kingdom to Israel and, instead, began preparing His disciples for His fast-approaching death and resurrection, teaching them how to carry on after He was gone. In Matthew 14—23, Jesus demonstrated His deity; revealed that God would offer the Kingdom to Gentiles, establishing a new organism—the church; and provided characteristics of the coming Kingdom through a series of parables. Then He was rejected for the final time.

DEMONSTRATION OF JESUS' DEITY

God's theocratic Kingdom will be ruled, of course, by God Himself through Messiah Jesus, the second Person of the triune Godhead. While on Earth, Jesus performed miracles that were designed to authenticate His identity and thereby His message. He raised the dead, quieted the seas, made the lame walk and the blind see, and demonstrated control over all the laws of nature.

Jesus didn't perform all these jaw-dropping miracles for no reason.

He did it to fulfill prophecy, so the Jewish people would be able to recognize that He was, indeed, their Messiah and know He was God. When Jesus heard His relative, John the Baptist, was beheaded, He took a boat and went "to a deserted place by Himself" (Mt. 14:13). But as soon as people realized where He had gone, He wasn't by Himself for long. Five thousand Jewish men arrived, along with women and children. Scripture says Jesus "healed their sick" (v. 14), which only the great Physician could do. Later, He fed them all using only five loaves of bread and two fish—normally not enough for two teenage boys. Yet He multiplied the food because He was *Jehovah Jireh*, the Lord who provides (Gen. 22:14), the Lord who takes what little we can offer Him and does something magnificent with it. Later He fed more than 4,000 Gentiles with merely seven loaves and "a few little fish" (Mt. 15:34). And everyone was satisfied.

Jesus also walked on water (14:25) because He is the God who created the laws of nature, "laid the foundations of the earth" (Job 38:4), and "shut in the sea with doors" (v. 8). He produced such spectacular signs and wonders that many people believed in Him and glorified the God of Israel (Mt. 15:31). Even the demons acknowledged who He was (Lk. 4:41).

But the Jewish leadership refused to believe Him despite all His miracles. The power-brokers of that day were the scribes, Pharisees, Sadducees, Herodians, and Zealots.

The scribes were responsible for meticulously copying and ultimately preserving the Jewish law. But they also were known for putting their own spin on it by adding manmade traditions that often contradicted the Lord's intent. The Pharisees (*Pharisee* is both Hebrew and Aramaic for "separated one") were religious leaders who conflicted with Jesus over the law and tried to trap Him into incriminating Himself as a lawbreaker.

The Zealots belonged to a political movement that worked to incite the Jewish people to rebel against the Roman Empire. The Herodians traditionally supported Herod the Great and his successors.

Generally, these groups strongly disliked one another and did not work well together. The one thing they all agreed on was that they hated Jesus. So when the scribes and Pharisees confronted Jesus, their mutual hatred for Him enabled them to team up. Jesus knew their hearts and hypocrisy and condemned their attempts to entrap Him and His followers.

Since the religious and political leaders wanted no part of Him, the offer of the Kingdom changed.

OFFER OF THE KINGDOM TO GENTILES

One of the first memory verses most people learn in church is John 3:16, and for good reason. It is chock-full of vital biblical truth: "For God so loved the world that He gave His only begotten Son, that whoever believes in Him should not perish but have everlasting life." This one verse tells us who (God) did what (gave His only Son), why He did it (because He loved the world), and who (whoever) must do what (believe in Him) to obtain something wonderful (everlasting life) and avoid something terrible (eternal death and condemnation).

John 3:16 pertains to everyone. It doesn't say, "For God so loved the Gentiles" or "For God so loved the Jewish people." It says, "For God so loved the world." When my wife, who was raised Jewish, was searching for the truth about Jesus, she read this verse and did what many others do: She inserted her name, after which she immediately became overcome with emotion because no one had ever told her God loved her.

It stands to reason God eventually would extend the Kingdom to the Gentiles. In fact, He told us so in the book of Isaiah, approximately 700 years before Messiah Jesus was born: "It is too small a thing that You should be My Servant to raise up the tribes of Jacob, and to restore the preserved ones of Israel; I will also give You as a light to the Gentiles, that You should be My salvation to the ends of the earth" (49:6).

When the Jewish leaders sealed their fate by rejecting Christ and His offer of the Kingdom, Jesus switched gears and began ministering to the Gentiles as well, beginning with a Syrophoenician woman in the Gentile region of Tyre and Sidon.

Addressing Jesus as "Lord, Son of David," the woman asked for healing for her "severely demon-possessed" daughter (Mt. 15:22). Her use of the Messianic title *Son of David* reflected her understanding that Jesus was Israel's Messiah. And her statement, "Even the little dogs eat the crumbs which fall from their masters' table" (v. 27), reflected her great faith. She understood that when Israel received its kingdom, blessing would trickle down to the Gentiles. She was simply asking that some of that residual blessing trickle down to her.

Unlike Israel's leaders, she knew and accepted Jesus for who He was after seeing the miracles He performed. As Jesus said, "Believe the works, that you may know and believe that the Father is in Me, and I in Him" (Jn. 10:38).

At first, the Lord's response to the woman seems a little disconcerting: "I was not sent, except to the lost sheep of the house of Israel" (Mt. 15:24). He had come to offer the physical sons of Jacob a literal Kingdom. It would have been inappropriate to bless the Gentiles before first blessing the Jewish people. But her reply demonstrated such amazing faith that Jesus not only healed her daughter but also declared, "O woman, great is your faith!" (v. 28).

Word must have spread quickly of His presence in the region, and large crowds flocked to hear His message and obtain healing for themselves and their loved ones. People, primarily Gentiles, "came to Him, having with them the lame, blind, mute, maimed, and many others; and they laid them down at Jesus' feet, and He healed them." Then they "glorified the God of Israel" (vv. 30–31).

The multitude stayed with Jesus on a mountain for three days. The disciples had just seen the Lord multiply fish and bread to feed five thousand Jewish men, plus women and children. Yet when Jesus told them He did not want to send this group away hungry because the people might faint, the disciples asked, "Where could we get enough bread in the wilderness to fill such a great multitude?" (v. 33). They still did not truly understand who He was or that He was completely capable of duplicating the miracle they witnessed days earlier.

This time He fed 4,000 men, plus women and children, with seven loaves and a few little fish. The miracle was as much a teaching tool for the disciples as it was a blessing for the hungry. Through it, He revealed the nature of the coming Kingdom: It would contain Jewish and Gentile believers who accepted Him by faith.

ESTABLISHMENT OF THE CHURCH

One of the most interesting places in Israel is Banias at the headwaters of the Jordan River. It is located near Caesarea Philippi, approximately 25 miles north of the Sea of Galilee at the base of Mount Hermon. Today it is a beautiful national park. In Jesus' day, however, the site was associated with the Greek god Pan, who was half-man, half-goat and often pictured playing a pan flute. It was a cesspool of vile, pagan worship that dated back to the third century BC.

There, in the shadow of debauchery so intense that the area was called the gates of hell, Jesus asked His disciples, "Who do men say that I, the Son of Man, am?" (Mt. 16:13). They replied by naming John the Baptist, Elijah, Jeremiah, or "one of the prophets" (v. 14). Then He asked, "But who do you say that I am?" (v. 15).

Speaking for the group, Simon Peter declared with amazing, God-given boldness, "You are the Christ, the Son of the living God" (v. 16). Jesus praised Peter's answer, telling him only the Father could have revealed that fact. Then He declared, "I also say to you that you are Peter, and on this rock I will build My church, and the gates of Hades shall not prevail against it" (v. 18).

For the first time, the Lord announced the creation of a new organism, His *ecclesia,* His called-out ones, the church. This body would be composed of Jews and Gentiles who understood the truth of Peter's statement, namely, that Jesus was the Christ, the Messiah, the Son of the God of Israel. On the "rock" of Peter's statement of faith, the new organism would be built.

Because the Jewish leadership rejected Christ, the Lord taught His disciples that He was passing the baton to the church, which now would carry the message of salvation to the world until the Rapture occurs and the church is removed. The nation of Israel was being set aside temporarily, and a new entity composed of all mankind was being born.

Jesus' next lesson taught His disciples about His approaching death and resurrection. He provided four key components of new revelation (v. 21): (1) He must go to Jerusalem. (2) In Jerusalem He would suffer many things at the hands of the Jewish religious leadership. (3) He would be killed; this is the first time in Matthew's Gospel that Jesus foretold His death. (4) He would be raised to life on the third day.

TEACHING ABOUT THE COMING KINGDOM

Three of the disciples—Peter, James, and John—experienced a small taste of what the future Kingdom will be like. Approximately a week after the feeding of the 4,000, Jesus took them up a high mountain, which many scholars identify as Mount Hermon, located in what today is the Golan Heights.

It was there that Jesus "was transfigured before them" (17:2). The word *transfigured* literally means "transformed." The Lord's face "shone like the sun, and His clothes became as white as the light." Moses and Elijah appeared and spoke with Jesus (vv. 2–3).

Moses may represent the period of the Exodus and Law, while Elijah possibly represents the prophets. The point is that both men are risen saints. The worldwide, Millennial Kingdom ruled by the risen, glorified Lord Jesus will be composed of risen saints who lived during the Old and New Testament periods; risen Church-Age saints; Tribulation saints; and mortal humans who survived the seven-year Tribulation and believed on Christ as their Savior.

The transfiguration was the literal fulfillment of Jesus' promise, "There are some standing here who shall not taste death till they see the Son of Man coming in His kingdom" (16:28). The three disciples saw Jesus glorified in a miniature, mountaintop kingdom.

This revelation later prompted the apostle John to declare, "And the Word became flesh and dwelt among us, and we beheld His glory, the glory as of the only begotten of the Father, full of grace and truth" (Jn. 1:14). The disciples beheld the glory of God, the glory of the divine Messiah-King who will one day rule the world and whose Kingdom will endure forever.

Jesus' incarnation did not alter the fact that He was 100 percent deity and, as such, possessed glory, a major attribute of God. Yet His glory was veiled by His body of flesh. At the Mount of Transfiguration, Christ's inner circle alone received a brief glimpse of this glory. However, when Jesus returns to establish His Kingdom, everyone will see Him arrive in glory as King of kings and Lord of lords (Rev. 19:16).

He will rule from David's throne, which probably will be located in the Holy of Holies in the Millennial Temple in Jerusalem because the prophet Zechariah declared,

> *Thus says the* Lord *of hosts, saying: "Behold, the Man whose name is the BRANCH! From His place He shall branch out, and He shall build the temple of the* Lord*; yes, He shall build the temple of the* Lord*. He shall bear the glory, and shall sit and rule on His throne; so He shall be a priest on His throne, and the counsel of peace shall be*

between them both" (Zech. 6:12–13).

After the transfiguration, Jesus gave crucial instruction to His disciples. He explained that having a relationship with the Father requires childlike faith and taught them they must be concerned for the lost. He explained how to handle discipline within the church and the necessity of having a heart that continually forgives others.

After a dialogue with a rich young ruler (Mt. 19:16–26), Peter asked what they as disciples would receive as rewards because they left everything and followed Him. Jesus replied, "Assuredly, I say to you, that in the regeneration, when the Son of Man sits on the throne of His glory, you who have followed Me will also sit on twelve thrones judging the twelve tribes of Israel" (vv. 27–28). The "regeneration" is the Millennial Kingdom, when Earth will be made new—regenerated, restored to its prefall condition.

This is an important revelation because Jesus was telling them unequivocally they will be ruling. If there were no Kingdom, what would they rule over? This verse is one of the clearest proofs of a future, literal Kingdom.

Jesus then began explaining characteristics of the coming Kingdom, beginning with a parable regarding recognition of and declaration to whom everyone must ultimately answer. Today we have a plethora of award ceremonies: Academy Awards, Tony Awards, Grammy Awards, Country Music Awards. The list seems endless as people honor one another. A day is coming when the rich, powerful, and popular of this world will find themselves being judged, not by their peers, but by the Judge of the whole earth. Many whom the world considered insignificant, useless, and unimportant will receive great reward for their faithfulness, while those highly esteemed today for their influence and talent may receive little reward in the Kingdom. When all is said and done, the Lord's opinion alone is the one that matters.

After sharing this parable, Jesus and His disciples began their journey to Jerusalem where the Lord would be betrayed "to the chief priests and to the scribes; and they will condemn Him to death, and deliver Him to the Gentiles" for crucifixion (20:18–19). While trying to prepare His followers for this fast-approaching trauma, James and John's mother requested special honor for her sons. Jesus used this awkward situation to explain why He came and to teach them humility and the need to esteem others better than themselves. The Lord does not want us to seek the preeminence but, rather, to emulate Him, who came not "to be served but to serve." He modeled the ultimate in servitude because He gave "His life a ransom for many" (v. 28).

FINAL REJECTION

From the outset, John the Baptist preached repentance for the King was coming. John was "the voice of one crying in the wilderness: 'Prepare the way of the LORD'" (Isa. 40:3). The entire purpose of his existence was to herald the coming King.

Jesus and His disciples ministered for three years, at the end of which the Jewish nation should have known exactly who Jesus was. At the so-called triumphal entry into Jerusalem, He presented Himself as their King, the rightful ruler of Israel. This event was foretold by the prophet Zechariah: "Rejoice greatly, O daughter of Zion! Shout, O daughter of Jerusalem! Behold, your King is coming to you" (Zech. 9:9). His arrival was a crescendo, the high point of His ministry declaring the Kingdom promise to Israel. He was literally fulfilling an ancient prophecy.

In ancient times, when a king was coming, workers were sent ahead to literally change the face of the ground on which the coming ruler would travel. They lowered mountains, filled valleys, and made the way as straight and level as possible. Jesus came to see if the hearts of His people were ready for His arrival. He came to see if the nation as a whole metaphorically had lowered the mountains, exalted the valleys, and was prepared for the arrival of its King. It was not prepared, primarily because of the power-brokers of the day, who despised Jesus. Although the rank and file shouted to Jesus, "Hosanna to the Son of David!" as He entered the city, the nation's religious and political leaders rejected Him (Mt. 21:9). They saw Him not as their rightful king, but as a usurper, troublemaker, and menace.

Jesus then condemned the scribes and Pharisees, calling them hypocrites, fools, and blind men. He declared Himself "the stone which the builders rejected" (21:42) and told them "the kingdom of God [the long-expected Millennial Kingdom] will be taken from you and given to a nation bearing the fruits of it" (v. 43).

Has Israel lost the reality of the Kingdom forever? Absolutely not!

The word *nation* as used here is better understood as "generation." That generation lost the Kingdom, but a future group of Jewish people will someday receive it. In fact, Jesus referred to that future generation when He lamented on the Mount of Olives: "O Jerusalem, Jerusalem the one who kills the prophets and stones those who are sent to her!...See! Your house is left to you desolate [empty]; for I say to you, you shall see Me no more till you say, 'Blessed is He who comes in the name of the Lord'" (23:37-39).

Someday, Israel will be betrayed by the Antichrist, the pseudo messiah with whom it will have entered into a seven-year treaty. When the nation's demise seems imminent, Jesus will return physically to this tortured planet and save Israel. The Jewish remnant of that day will be the one that shouts, "Hosanna [save now]! Blessed is He who comes in the name of the Lord."

Those people will look on Him "whom they have pierced" (Zech. 12:10); and they will be the ones—not the church (it will rule with Jesus) and not the Gentiles—who will inherit the Kingdom. It has always been and will always be a Jewish Kingdom. But Gentiles are privileged to enter into it, by God's grace. And together we can say, "Hallelujah!"

CHAPTER ELEVEN

God's Kingdom in the Olivet Discourse

Steve Herzig

Ani Ma'amin, "I believe," is part of Jewish liturgy recited at the end of the morning prayers. Of the thirteen principles of faith Maimonides[1] wrote, number 12 states, "I believe with perfect faith in the coming of the Messiah, and even though he should tarry, I nevertheless will wait every day for his coming."

Belief in a personal Messiah and the hope of his coming is at the core of observant Jewish thought. Maimonides wrote, "Whoever does not believe in him (Messiah), or does not await his coming, denies not only [the statements of] the other prophets, but also [those of] the Torah and of Moses, our teacher, for the Torah attests to his coming."[2] Observant Jews believe several things will occur when Messiah comes: He will bring Jews scattered around the world back to the land of Israel, he will help to rebuild the holy Temple, He will usher in peace to all the world, and he will end sin and evil.

These results of the Messiah's coming according to Orthodox Judaism are similar to what Bible-believing Christians expect. This agreement is not surprising. Both believe Messiah fulfills the writings of the prophets, who painted an optimistic future for the nation of Israel and its people. However, Christianity holds a fundamentally different view of the person of the Messiah and the number of times He comes. Hebrews 9:28 sums it up: "So Christ was offered once to bear the sins of many. To those who eagerly wait for Him He will appear a second time, apart from sin, for salvation." The writer of Hebrews was Jewish, writing to Jewish people who believed Jesus is the God-Man, Messiah.

In looking forward to God's coming Kingdom, we need to understand

Jesus' teaching in what we call the Olivet Discourse in Matthew 24 and 25.

As background, Jesus had just celebrated Passover with His disciples. In only a few hours, He would be beaten, rejected, humiliated, murdered, and hung on a cross. Oblivious to what was to come, His disciples had questions about the timing of the future Kingdom. To answer them, He delivered His longest prophetic message recorded in the Bible.

This message "reveals His interpretation of crucial Old Testament prophetic passages concerning Israel and the nations and serves as an inspired master outline of end-times events. Furthermore, it explains God's judgment on Israel, especially His promised restoration of it at the advent of King Messiah and the establishment of His Messianic rule."[3] It also serves as a template for future New Testament teaching that will detail His sudden, unexpected, visible, powerful, glorious, and triumphant return to establish His Kingdom.

THE COMING KING'S ARRIVAL (MATTHEW 24:29–36)

The King is coming—but when? Jesus said, "Immediately after the tribulation of those days" (v. 29). The first twenty-eight verses of Matthew 24 detail Daniel's 70th week. We call this period the Tribulation when cosmic disturbances will occur: "The sun will be darkened, and the moon will not give its light; the stars will fall from heaven, and the powers of the heavens will be shaken" (v. 29). The universe will convulse to ensure everyone alive pays attention.

After those cosmic changes, "the sign of the Son of Man will appear in heaven" (v. 30), which I believe is the Shekinah Glory of God. This is the same Glory the Israelites saw in their flight from Egypt; the same Glory Moses saw when he received the Law; the same Glory Peter, James, and John saw when Jesus was transfigured in front of them (17:2). The apostle John described it this way: "He is coming with clouds, and every eye will see Him" (Rev. 1:7).

John further described Jesus' Second Coming in Revelation 19: "I saw heaven opened, and behold, a white horse" (v. 11). The appearance of the horse's rider will be awesome in the true sense of the word. His "eyes were like a flame of fire" (v. 12), His robe is "dipped in blood" (v. 13), and "out of His mouth goes a sharp sword" (v. 15). According to the prophet Daniel, His coming will be sudden, glorious, and with power (Dan. 7:13–14). When He comes He gathers "His elect," Israel, "from the four winds" (Mt. 24:31).

The prophets foretold that the Jewish people would be scattered: "All of you who remain I will scatter to all the winds" (Ezek. 5:10). "I have spread you abroad like the four winds of heaven" (Zech. 2:6). But they will be regathered at the coming of the King: "He...will gather together the dispersed of Judah from the four corners of the earth" (Isa. 11:12). The Lord God beckons His people to "come from the four winds" (Ezek. 37:9). There never was, nor will there ever be, a more amazing, glorious, or spectacular event than the coming of the King to Earth as He gathers His elect.

The parable of the fig tree in Matthew 24:32–35 also helps us project the timing of Jesus' coming. The word *parable* comes from two Greek words, *para* and *ballo*, which together mean "to throw alongside." It is a literary device Jesus often used to teach something new. In his book on Jesus' parables, John Butler wrote, "A parable is a picture, not a precept. A parable depicts a doctrine, it does not determine a doctrine. Also, not every detail in a parable is given to teach some important truth but often is there to simply help the flow and continuity of the parable."[4]

This parable communicates one simple fact: When a fig tree displayed tender branches and emerging leaves, it indicated summer was coming. The sign, then, is that "when you see all these things" (v. 33), you know Jesus' coming is near. Jesus put it this way in Luke's account: "Now when these things begin to happen, look up and lift up your heads, because your redemption draws near" (Lk. 21:28).

Jesus explained that the people living to see "these things" won't pass away until they are fulfilled. The word *generation* (Greek, *genea*) used in Matthew 24:34 can mean race, nation, or age and can also refer to a physical or moral span of time. The generation that sees all these signs will know for certain Christ could return at any moment. So it appears the word *generation* refers to Jews and Gentiles who will be alive when "all these things" take place. Thus, Jesus said the generation that witnesses all the Tribulation events will be the generation that also witnesses His Second Coming (Mt. 24:4–31; cf. Rev. 6—19).[5]

WATCHING FOR THE KING'S ARRIVAL (MATTHEW 25:1–13)

After telling the parable of the fig tree, Jesus told another parable, this one about ten virgins. In the context of a Jewish wedding, the virgins were bridesmaids, attendants to the bride.

Weddings were different in the first century than today. A number of formal steps were taken. First, the marriage was arranged, usually through the parents or a matchmaker. Once the agreement was reached, the groom's family paid a dowry to the bride's family. Next was the betrothal when the couple exchanged vows and two witnesses signed a marriage contract called a *ketubah*, which was protection for the bride by outlining the husband's responsibilities. Once signed, the couple was officially married. The only way the marriage could dissolve was by death or divorce. The consummation of the marriage occurred later.

In the meantime, the groom went back alone to his father's house and prepared a place for his wife. The third step is the marriage feast. Sometime after the betrothal, which lasted a minimum of a year, at an appointed time the groom made his way to the bride's house, accompanied by his attendants; the blowing of trumpets; and the proclamation, "Behold, the bridegroom is coming!" In the meantime, the bride was watching and waiting for her groom, though in this parable Jesus didn't mention the bride. The focus is clearly on the bridesmaids who were watching and waiting for the bridegroom.

Jesus divided the ten bridesmaids into two groups. Five were wise, and five were foolish (v. 2). Five had extra oil for their lamps, while five had only the oil in their lamps (vv. 3–4). Since Matthew started this parable with the word *then*, we can assume the Tribulation theme of the previous verses is the context of the story. The bridesmaids knew the bridegroom was coming, but they didn't know when, probably why they "slumbered and slept" (v. 5).

When they heard the midnight call, they all responded by trimming their lamps (vv. 6–7). The foolish, unprepared bridesmaids asked the others to give them oil because their lamps were going out. But the wise, prepared bridesmaids would not share their oil, knowing there would not be enough for all of them (vv. 8–9). So the foolish bridesmaids were forced to leave to buy more oil, a difficult task at midnight.

While they were away, the bridegroom arrived (v. 10). The wise bridesmaids were ready with extra oil to keep their lamps burning and were able to go to the wedding feast. However, the five foolish bridesmaids missed their opportunity; by the time they returned, "the door was shut" (v. 10). They pleaded, "Lord, Lord, open to us!" but the bridegroom answered, "I do not know you" (v. 11).

The ten bridesmaids represent Israel in the Tribulation period, waiting for the Messiah. Not all of them were prepared. The five wise bridesmaids represent believers who, according to Amos 4:12, were prepared to meet their God. They carried extra oil. In Scripture, oil often represents the Holy Spirit.[6] Thus, these five were prepared because they believed the message of the Kingdom preached during the 70th week of Daniel and entered the Kingdom (Mt. 24). The foolish bridesmaids were not believers and, thus, unprepared and unequipped for the bridegroom's arrival. They did not enter the Kingdom.

Matthew 25:13 records a solemn warning: "Watch therefore, for you know neither the day nor the hour in which the Son of Man is coming." Watching and preparing for His coming are two keys to this parable. During the Tribulation, the message of the Kingdom will be preached. Certainly, many Jewish people will watch for the King to come; but only those Jewish people who have the oil, who believe in *Yeshua* (Jesus), will be prepared to enter the Kingdom.

Ani Ma'amin, "I believe," is not enough unless one is prepared. Jesus said, "My sheep hear My voice, and I know them, and they follow Me" (Jn. 10:27). Not all Israel is saved Israel (Rom. 9:6). Only those who receive and believe the true Messiah and King are able to enter in to the feast.

WORKING UNTIL THE KING'S ARRIVAL (MATTHEW 25:14–30)

There is an art to waiting. Check out a typical mall today; and you probably will see numerous men sitting on benches, legs crossed, and shopping bags on their laps, waiting for their wives. They are not doing anything. The art of waiting is to be occupied while you wait. The parable of the talents is a great example of working while waiting.

The word *for* (v. 14) connects this parable to the previous one about the bridesmaids. Watching and preparing is the lesson of the bridesmaids while working and performing is the key to the parable of the talents. While we wait for the King, we must work and produce for Him in His absence.

A man who was going out of town "delivered his goods" to three servants (v. 14). The goods he gave were in the form of talents, a coin worth about 60 minas. A mina was the equivalent of a day's wages. One servant received five talents, one received two talents, and the third received one talent. The number of talents given was "according to his own ability" (v.15). The master then left the country.

The first man invested his five talents, doubling them to ten. The second servant also doubled his talents from two to four. The third servant dug a hole in the ground and "hid his lord's money" (v. 18). When the master returned, he "came and settled accounts with them" (v. 19). He praised the first two servants, "Well done, good and faithful servant; you were faithful over a few things, I will make you ruler over many things. Enter into the joy of your lord" (v. 21; cf. v. 23).

However, the third servant was not so fortunate. Since he hid away his talent, it didn't increase; thus, his master called him "unprofitable" (v. 30). The servant had an explanation for why he hid it, saying, "I knew you to be a hard man, reaping where you have not sown, and gathering where you have not scattered seed. And I was afraid" (vv. 24–25). As a result, his lord called him "wicked and lazy," explaining he could have "deposited my money with the bankers, and at my coming I would have received back my own with interest" (vv. 26–27). The master then took the talent from the third servant and gave it to the servant who turned five talents into ten. The unprofitable servant was then cast into outer darkness where "there will be weeping and gnashing of teeth" (v. 30).

The master saw the two servants who doubled their talents as worthy because they used the talents they were given and increased their value. They were faithful. Though the two servants had a differing amount of talents, they provided their master the same return, doubling their value. They used what they were given. But the third servant who said his master was hard did not invest at all. If he really was afraid, why did he not act? As a result, his master judged him as unworthy, called him out as "unprofitable," and cast him away (vv. 26, 30). His judgment should serve as a warning to us.

Unbelievers are unprofitable servants who are separated from God. The call to you now is, "Believe on the Lord Jesus Christ, and you will be saved" (Acts 16:31). The call in the Tribulation is, "Watch! Prepare! Believe!" People who don't know the King will be judged and cast into the lake of fire at the end of the Kingdom period (Rev. 20:15).

Believers waiting for the King and believers today have a responsibility to work while waiting for Him. God gives all believers talents, something of value. He gifts us all but not all the same. What are we doing with those talents? "For we must all appear before the judgment seat of Christ, that each one may receive the things done in the body, according to what he has done, whether good or bad" (2 Cor. 5:10). The faithful servants were judged by their production, by their work, not by how much they gave. Are you using the talents God has given you?

Gentiles will be judged on the basis of their treatment of Jesus' kinsmen (Mt. 25:31–46). Jesus told His disciples that He, the Son of Man, is coming. This is not a theory. Jesus said, "*When* the Son of Man comes" (v. 31, emphasis added). Know this, He is coming; and the Person coming is not only King, but God, the Creator and Sustainer of all things. When He comes, He will judge Israel. He will redeem His people as He promised. It will happen with "all the holy angels," and He will "sit on the throne of His glory" (v. 31). Though He will sit on David's throne and rule the Kingdom, the throne mentioned here is not David's. That throne is in Jerusalem.

This throne is different. Joel 3:2 says, "I will also gather all nations, and bring them down to the Valley of Jehoshaphat," which today is called the Kidron Valley, located between the Mount of Olives and the Temple Mount. "All the nations will be gathered before Him, and he will separate them as a shepherd divides his sheep from the goats" (Mt. 25:32). These nations are Gentles, individual people.

The sheep—the righteous ones—will be on Jesus' right; and He will say to them, "Come, you blessed of My Father, inherit the kingdom prepared for you from the foundation of the world" (vv. 33–34). On His left are the goats—the unrighteous, unbelievers—to whom He will say, "Depart from Me, you cursed, into the everlasting fire prepared for the devil and his angels (v. 41).

The timing of this judgment is right after Jesus returns to Earth. The basis of this judgment is how Gentiles treated the Lord's brethren. Who are they? They are the persecuted Jewish people, living and suffering in the Tribulation. The sheep on the right are righteous Gentiles who will feed and clothe them, give them drink, take them in, visit them when they are sick and in prison (vv. 35–36). They are surprised to find that the way they treated Jesus' people is counted as how they treated Him.

Surprised also are the goats, or unbelievers. Their mistreatment of suffering Jewish people in the Tribulation is regarded by the Lord as mistreatment against Him. No doubt, righteous Gentiles will emerge at the preaching of the 144,000 Jewish evangelists God will raise up in the Tribulation period (Rev. 7:4). They will bring about the salvation of a great host of Gentiles from every tribe, kindred, nation, and tongue (v. 9).

CONCLUSION

Jesus' lengthy sermon—the longest recorded for us—drives home important truths. It also provides encouragement for the disciples whom He privately addressed, for us today, and for those in the Tribulation period in the future. Here is the message: Jesus the King is coming again. When He comes, there will be such an incredible display of power and glory that the heavens convulse in displaying it.

His followers should be watching for Him, waiting for Him, and preparing for Him, all the while using the resources He gives us and investing them in the work of the ministry.

This sermon also illustrates that Genesis 12:3 is always in play: "I will bless those who bless you, and I will curse him who curses you; and in you all the families of the earth shall be blessed."

Even so, come, Lord Jesus!

CHAPTER TWELVE

God's Kingdom in Acts and the Epistles

Chris Katulka

Most people look forward to their birthdays (unless they've decided they're not getting older!) or Christmas with great anticipation. These special days often come with presents and parties, special meals and cards—something to look forward to. But this anticipation pales in comparison with looking forward to the coming of God's Kingdom; or at least it should.

The study on God's Kingdom thus far has taken us on a journey through the Old Testament and into the Gospels, highlighting the great anticipation for the realization of the Kingdom on Earth. The tension that exists from Adam and Eve's fall in the Garden of Eden, when sin entered the world, to the Bethlehem birth of Jesus, Israel's Redeemer, is palpable. One easily could read through the Law, prophets, and writings of the Old Testament and get a basic sense of the Messianic and spiritual void that prevented God's Kingdom from becoming a reality.

When Jesus was born, His arrival was expected to accomplish what the Old Testament prophets promised: "consolation of Israel" (Lk. 2:25), restoration of Israel's Kingdom to its former glory, suppression of their enemies, and the Messianic Age that would put Israel above the nations of the world. When you finish reading Jesus' birth story in Matthew and Luke, you're left feeling that God is at work and want to shout, "This is the One!"

Even Jesus' ministry on Earth points to His Messianic authority as He lived out the true heart of God's Law with His people. He healed the sick, raised the dead, and taught in synagogues about the Kingdom. However, the oligarchy in charge of the religious and political life of

Israel was threatened by Jesus' profound influence on the people. The very people Jesus came to offer the Kingdom to were the same ones who rejected Him, ultimately leading to His death. The anticipated King of Israel was crucified and buried.

The Gospel of Luke, written by the same author as the book of Acts, ends on the road to Emmaus, with two disciples saying, "We were hoping that it was He who was going to redeem Israel" (24:21). Little did the two disciples know they were talking to the resurrected Jesus!

Luke continues the narrative in the book of Acts. He, along with the authors of the Epistles, stressed that Jesus' death was no hiccup in God's plan. In fact, His resurrection validated every word and deed He said and did during His earthly ministry. For forty days after His resurrection, Jesus met with His disciples and taught them about the Kingdom of God (Acts 1:3). After this special and unique time with His disciples, Jesus ascended to heaven to sit at the right hand of the Father.

For nearly eight centuries, Jewish prophets predicted the coming of the One who would rebuild the "tabernacle of David" (Amos 9:11). After so many years of waiting, it seemed as though the Son of David and His Kingdom were finally ready to burst on the scene. Yet Jesus' ascension to heaven, which almost seems to mimic God's departure from the Temple in Ezekiel's vision from the Mount of Olives (Ezek. 9—11), leaves the disciples to ask the question, "What now?"

KINGDOM COME OR KINGDOM COMING (ACTS)

As the disciples interacted with the risen and glorified Messiah after His resurrection, they probably felt confident that Jesus would establish the Kingdom of God and restore Israel's fortunes. Jesus spent the better part of forty days teaching them about the Kingdom. In the beginning of the book of Acts, Luke set the scene with Jesus and His disciples on the Mount of Olives.

For the disciples, this was the opportune time and place to usher in the Kingdom. They probably were familiar with the prophetic significance of the Mount of Olives, so they asked, "Lord, will You at this time restore the kingdom to Israel?" (Acts 1:6). Jesus responded, "It is not for you to know times or seasons which the Father has put in His own authority. But you shall receive power when the Holy Spirit has come upon you; and you shall be witnesses to Me in Jerusalem, and in all Judea and Samaria, and to the end of the earth" (1:7–8).

The disciples' question to Jesus is a defining one that will lay a foundation for how readers of the book of Acts and the Epistles understand the Kingdom of God in the Church Age. There are varying opinions among New Testament scholars on Jesus' response to their inquiry.

For instance, sixteenth-century reformer John Calvin believed it was foolish for the disciples to ask Jesus such a mundane question about the Kingdom:

There are as many errors in this question as words. They ask him as concerning a kingdom; but they dream of an earthly kingdom.... Now, they hoped for the restoring hereof at the coming of the Messias [sic], and hereupon was it that so soon as the apostles saw their Master Christ risen from the dead, they straightway began to think thereupon; but, in the meantime, they declared thereby how bad scholars they were under so good a Master.[1]

It's quite bold of Calvin to call the apostles bad scholars since for Calvin—and other modern scholars who agree with him—the definition of Israel developed into the church in Acts and the Epistles. Also, the term *Kingdom* moved, in their opinion, from a territorial kingdom in the Old Testament to a spiritual one in Christ. Calvin, like many reformers of his time, underestimated the role national Israel plays in God's plan of redemption.

F. F. Bruce argued, "The kingdom of God...which they were commissioned to proclaim was the Good News of God's grace in Christ. Their present question appears to have been the last flicker of their former burning expectation of an imminent theocracy with themselves as its chief executives."[2] Bruce believed this was the moment the disciples left behind their expectations for what the prophets promised, and they moved forward to a more enlightened understanding of God's Kingdom.

Bruce was correct. The disciples did put aside their political ambitions to be King of Israel's right-hand men. However, the disciples throughout Acts and the Epistles ministered the Good News of God's grace in Christ with a sense of urgency, knowing that His return could happen at any moment and would bring the Kingdom. That's why Peter wrote in his first letter, "But the end of all things is at hand; therefore be serious and watchful in your prayers" (1 Pet. 4:7).

Jesus never rebuked the disciples' question of Israel's future liberation, and He spent forty days talking with them about the Kingdom. So their question probably wasn't off base. The way Jesus responded to the questions shows agreement; He, too, wanted the Kingdom restored to Israel. However, He drew the focus away from the when of the Kingdom to the how by giving them their mission to be witnesses in Jerusalem, Judea, Samaria, and the end of the earth by the Holy Spirit's power.

In Acts 2, the Holy Spirit indwelled believers on Pentecost; and the church was born. Following this event, Peter and John began to minister in the Temple complex. The two healed a lame man, and the people in the area gathered to see what happened. Peter took advantage of the moment to point to Jesus, calling for the Jewish people around him to

repent therefore and be converted, that your sins may be blotted out, so that times of refreshing may come from the presence of the Lord, and that He may send Jesus Christ, who was preached to you before, whom heaven must receive until the times of restoration of all things, which God has spoken by the mouth of all His holy prophets since the world began (Acts 3:19–21).

Peter's gospel message to the Jewish audience at the Temple unearthed three theological truths about the Kingdom in its present form during the Church Age and the how of God's coming Kingdom:

1. In his sermon, Peter clearly communicated that Jesus was put to death out of ignorance. Ignorance doesn't alleviate the Jewish people of their sin; but God, in His mercy, extends His grace, calling them to repentance with the promise of forgiveness in the name of Jesus. Ultimately, Peter was communicating that God was not finished with Israel. There was still the promise of restoration through repentance, but they must make a decision to believe in Him.
2. Peter's message was both a call to the nation of Israel and an appeal to the individual to respond to God's gracious offer. Jewish thought leading up to the first century taught that the repentance of the nation of Israel as a whole, or even a large portion of the nation, could kick-start the "times of refreshing" and "restoration of all things."[3] This collective Jewish sense of ushering in the Messianic Age is even found

in rabbinical tradition, which teaches that if every Jewish person honored the Sabbath globally, then Messiah would appear.[4] Peter called the nation to repentance with the understanding that corporately they could bring blessing to the whole world through their faith in Messiah Jesus.
3. Peter's sermon also reveals that even during the Church Age, a restoration of the promised Kingdom from the Old Testament was still anticipated. Peter used the same word, *restoration*, in Acts 3:21 that's found in Acts 1:6, when the disciples asked their poignant question to Jesus, "Lord, will You at this time restore the kingdom to Israel?" It's vital to keep in mind that when the disciples asked Christ whether now was the time He would restore the Kingdom to Israel, it was prior to the coming of the Holy Spirit and the establishment of the church. Peter's message in the Temple was given after the events of Acts 2, which shows the restoration of an earthly kingdom is still on the minds of the disciples as they shared the Good News of Jesus Christ. Also, Peter's hope wasn't an alteration of the Kingdom because of the resurrection of Christ; it was a hope of Israel's restoration based on what the Old Testament prophets promised (3:21).

Jewish acceptance and belief in Jesus as Israel's Messiah is the hinge to the establishment of God's Kingdom on Earth as seen in Peter's sermon early in Acts. This theme continues as the narrative transitions away from Jerusalem to the "ends of the earth" with the ministry of the apostle Paul.

Paul's calling to minister to the Gentiles fits perfectly within the prophets' anticipation of future Kingdom restoration. Paul was a scholar of the Old Testament; and he knew God gave Daniel insights into His coming Kingdom, against the backdrop of the rise and fall of earthly kingdoms. In Daniel's prophecy, peoples, nations, and languages would serve the promised Messiah, the Son of Man. God's restoration of the Kingdom was not only for Israel; it was also for the benefit of the nations. Israel's purpose was to be a conduit of spiritual and physical blessing to the world (Gen. 12:3). That's why Paul took the Good News of Jesus Christ to the "ends of the earth."

Yet, even though Paul's mission was to the Gentiles, he still saw the eschatological value of reaching the Jewish community in the Diaspora. Paul's custom was to visit the synagogue before he ministered to the Gentiles. He visited synagogues and Jewish leaders in all the major cities of the Mediterranean world: Salamis, Antioch, Iconium, Thessalonica, Berea, Athens, Corinth, Ephesus, and Rome.

Throughout the book of Acts, Luke maintained the prophetic role of Israel and the hope of its redemption, which would usher in restoration.[5] Acts concludes with Paul appealing his case of heresy for preaching salvation through Christ before Caesar in Rome. At a glance, the trajectory of Acts almost seems to lead the reader away from Jerusalem and its prophetic significance; but it's crucial to remember why Paul fought to get to Rome. He wanted to state his case before Caesar, the representative of the Gentile world, in the hub of the Gentile world, Rome.

Paul was in Rome for one reason: to preach Messiah Jesus and the coming of God's Kingdom. He was going to point Caesar not to Rome, but to Jerusalem, where the King of kings would return and establish His rule over the nations. When Jesus commanded the disciples to go from Jerusalem to Judea, Samaria, and the ends of the Earth, He didn't draw a line out from Jerusalem. Instead, He drew circles around it. The center of the bullseye was Jerusalem.

DIVINE JUDGMENT AND THE COMING KINGDOM (EPISTLES)

The same anticipation and longing for God's Kingdom in Acts also is seen throughout the Epistles. Passages that stress Christ's Second Coming (2 Th. 2:8; Ti. 2:13), the resurrection of the saints (1 Cor. 15; Phil. 3:20–21), and the future inheritance of the Kingdom (Eph. 1:14; Eph. 5:5) have Israel's restoration embedded in them.

Another indication in the Epistles that the Kingdom was not yet realized is the clear contrast that exists between the spiritual position of those believers in Christ and unbelievers who are controlled by the worldly system. Paul, who was fully aware of the authority given to Jesus by the Father, still noted that Satan has dominion over the world (Eph. 2:2–3). John, in his first epistle, also drew a contrast between people who follow God and everyone else who is under the control of Satan who rules the world (1 Jn. 5:19). Finally, Peter encouraged believers to stay alert because Satan is still seeking to devour God's people (1

Pet. 5:8). All these passages portray an environment that is hostile to Christians, opposite the condition of God's Kingdom.

We need to read the Epistles through the lens of unfulfilled prophetic events and how Christians should live in light of Christ's return. For people in Christ, the full inheritance and blessing of God's Kingdom will be experienced at Christ's Second Coming. However, for those who have neglected to place their faith in Jesus, their inheritance is God's judgment.

For example, the prophet Malachi completed his prophecy with a cliffhanger for the restoration of Israel. The reader knows things aren't as they should be, and God is going to fix everything through the coming of the Messiah and divine judgment. Malachi considered God's judgment to be a refiner's fire (Mal. 3:2), launderer's soap (v. 2), and burning oven (4:1). The coming of God's Kingdom for some people will be considered "the great and dreadful day of the Lord" (4:5).

The prophet Zephaniah recorded God's words: "I will bring distress upon men, And they shall walk like blind men, because they have sinned against the Lord; their blood shall be poured out like dust, and their flesh like refuse" (Zeph. 1:17). The prophets often pronounced God's judgment, and through that judgment Kingdom restoration would give way. For instance, Zephaniah predicted God's wrath. Yet at the end of his book, he wrote, "'At that time I will bring you back, even at the time I gather you; for I will give you fame and praise among all the peoples of the earth, when I return your captives before your eyes,' says the Lord" (3:20). Therefore, divine judgment on sin precedes God's Kingdom.

Epistle writers like Peter and Paul employed the same prophetic call in their letters. The difference, however, is Jesus. The promised Messiah had come and now is sitting at the Father's right hand.

Paul opened his letter to the church in Rome by arguing that God's divine judgment is being revealed and will be poured out on all unrighteousness and ungodliness. Paul leveled the playing field in the beginning of Romans. Being Jewish or Gentile doesn't matter. Sin plagues all mankind, and God's creation must be purified from it: "For the wrath of God is revealed from heaven against all ungodliness and unrighteousness of men" (Rom. 1:18). Here Paul described how God's wrath is both presently and prophetically functioning.

God's wrath is presently displayed when He permits people to choose the way of sin and all its consequences. God "gave them up" to their dishonorable passions (v. 24); the consequence of their sin is a present sign of God's judgment. Simultaneously, each of those present sins also is stored up for the day of wrath when God judges the world: "But in accordance with your hardness and your impenitent heart you are treasuring up for yourself wrath in the day of wrath and revelation of the righteous judgment of God" (2:5). Paul was building his case that all people, Jewish and Gentile, need a Savior to deliver them from present and future judgment.

Peter, like Paul, also envisioned a divine judgment that must occur before God's Kingdom arrives. God's imminent judgment is in concert with Christ's Second Coming. That's why Peter said "the day of the Lord" could happen at any moment like a "thief in the night" (2 Pet. 3:10). The heavens and Earth will experience the full force of God's wrath, and all of mankind's works will be laid bare.

Peter then explained that after God's divine judgment, we are to look for "new heavens and a new earth," as God promised (v. 13). Also, God's judgment purifies the world from sin to welcome what would become the essence of God's Kingdom rule, righteousness.

ISRAEL'S REPENTANCE AND THE COMING KINGDOM (EPISTLES)

The prophets repeatedly reminded Israel that deliverance and restoration could be realized through repentance. The prophet Hosea wrote, "O Israel, return to the LORD your God, for you have stumbled because of your iniquity; take words with you, and return to the LORD. Say to Him, 'Take away all iniquity; receive us graciously, for we will offer the sacrifices of our lips'" (Hos. 14:1–2). God was calling Israel, who cheated on Him by embracing idol worship, to return to Him and find forgiveness and acceptance.

When Peter preached to the crowd of Jewish onlookers, he encouraged his audience to repent and trust in Jesus as Israel's Messiah. Jewish repentance would be the impetus for restoring the Kingdom to Israel (Acts 3:21). Paul was in lockstep with Peter's message. The apostle to the Gentiles knew Israel's repentance would usher in a period of blessing not only for Israel, but for the entire world.

Paul's letter to the Romans has a unique section that gives definition to Israel's unique role in God's plan of redemption despite their rejection of Jesus. Paul opened Romans 9—11 with a wish to see his brothers in the flesh, the Jewish people, come to faith in Christ:

> *I tell the truth in Christ, I am not lying, my conscience also bearing me witness in the Holy Spirit, that I have great sorrow and continual grief in my heart. For I could wish that I myself were accursed from Christ for my brethren, my countrymen according to the flesh, who are Israelites, to whom pertain the adoption, the glory, the covenants, the giving of the law, the service of God, and the promises; of whom are the fathers and from whom, according to the flesh, Christ came, who is over all, the eternally blessed God. Amen* (9:1–5).

Paul's longing for his people to come to faith in the Messiah was rooted in his desire to see God's Kingdom become a reality. In Romans 8, Paul wrote that "creation eagerly waits for the revealing of the sons of God" (v. 19). God's creation is eagerly anticipating resurrection and the coming of His Kingdom when righteousness reigns. Paul knew that Israel's salvation is the hinge that opens the door to God's Kingdom. That's why he opened Romans 9—11 with his wish to see the Jewish people come to faith in Messiah Jesus. It meant so much to him that he even was willing to sacrifice his relationship with Christ to ensure Israel would repent and believe Jesus is the Messiah.

Paul's prayer in the beginning of Romans 9 is reminiscent of Moses' prayer after the golden calf incident (Ex. 32). Moses interceded on behalf of Israel and said, "Yet now, if You will forgive their sin—but if not, I pray, blot me out of Your book which You have written" (v. 32).

Again, Paul wanted to communicate to the church in Rome that Jerusalem and the Jewish people still matter and Jesus' death and resurrection were no mistake in God's plan of redemption: "For if their being cast away is the reconciling of the world, what will their acceptance be but life from the dead?" (Rom. 11:15). Israel's disbelief in Jesus created the window of opportunity to reconcile the Gentile world to God, a reason to rejoice in God's grace.

However, God is not through yet. The best is yet to come! Paul compared and contrasted our Christian experience through the lens of Israel's belief in Jesus. When Israel accepts Jesus and believes physical resurrection will occur, they will experience "life from the dead."

Resurrection and God's Kingdom go hand in hand; you cannot fully enter into the Kingdom until you're resurrected.

Paul's confidence in God's promises and Israel's salvation compelled him to write to the church in Rome that one day "all Israel will be saved" (11:26). One day everyone in Israel, which has been backed against the wall by the nations of the world, will encounter their Deliverer: "They will look on Me whom they pierced" and repent and turn to the Savior (Zech. 12:10).

Rome isn't the centerpiece of God's plan because "the Deliverer will come out of Zion, and He will turn away ungodliness from Jacob; for this is My covenant with them, when I take away their sins" (Rom. 11:26–27). The centerpiece of God's Kingdom remains Israel's Messiah, Jesus, and Jerusalem, the capital of God's reign on Earth.

The Second Coming of Jesus serves as both divine judgment on sin and Israel's repentance in unison.

CONCLUSION

Acts and the Epistles often can be viewed as divergences from God's Kingdom agenda laid out by the Old Testament prophets. However, from the beginning of the church, the apostles saw that God was still executing His plan to bring the Kingdom "on earth as it is in heaven." They had clarity about God's Kingdom because the King had come and is coming again.

Like the apostles, we are still waiting for God's Kingdom. But are we looking forward to it with the same anticipation?

CHAPTER THIRTEEN

Controversial Teachings on the Kingdom

Mike Stallard

Although Christians agree on essentials of the faith, such as the triune God, Jesus' death and bodily resurrection, and salvation from sin through faith in Christ alone, they disagree in some areas of theology. One of these is the character and timing of God's Kingdom.

God's Kingdom prominently occurs in the Bible. If you include the Kingdom parables in the Gospels, it's the most frequent topic Jesus covered in His teaching ministry. An inductive study throughout Scripture on this topic would have to include words like *king, kingdom, rule, ruler, prince,* and *head.*

HISTORY OF CONTROVERSIAL TEACHINGS

After a thorough study, three major categories of Kingdom emerge: (1) God rules in general sovereignty over all that is in the universe all the time (Dan. 2:47; 4:3). (2) Christ reigns as Head of the church (Eph. 1:22–23). This is largely a spiritual reign in and through believers in the present age by means of God's Spirit. (3) When Christ returns a second time, He will establish an earthly Kingdom centered in Israel (Isa. 11; Zech. 14; Rev. 19—20). He is coming as the Messianic, Davidic King of Israel.

This Kingdom is a fulfillment of the promises given to Israel, especially in the Davidic Covenant. Throughout history, professing Christians rarely doubt the first category. However, the third one often is rejected by people who have no place in their theology for a future national Israel, even though it is the most-emphasized aspect of Kingdom teaching in the Bible.

Most believers in the early church held to chiliasm.[1] This word is the old way of saying Premillennialism, the belief that Christ will return to establish His earthly Kingdom. In spite of this correct approach to biblical teaching early on, the church began to wander from the truth about the nature of God's promised Kingdom.

Several factors led to this decline. First, the destruction of Jerusalem and the Temple in AD 70 by the Roman armies made some Christians wonder if God had turned His back on the Jewish people. As a result, the Jewish character of the coming, earthly Kingdom began to be doubted in spite of its biblical truth. Included in this change was the hint of rising anti-Semitism within the church.[2] Second, in the second century, the resurgence of Platonic thinking reinforced a nonliteral understanding of the Kingdom. Platonic thinking emphasizes the idea of something, not the concrete reality of it. The concept of the Kingdom began to morph into a spiritual, mystical Kingdom, rather than an earthly one. Third, the rise of Gnosticism added the idea that material things were evil; only spiritual, mystical things led to true understanding. All of these factors combined to downplay any coming, concrete, earthly Kingdom centered in Israel.

The church began to replace Israel in the minds of most Christians. This change usually meant that the blessings to Israel, even promises of a future land and Kingdom, were changed to spiritual promises only for the church today. It is interesting that the curses on Israel from the Old Testament do not seem to be applied to the church in most Replacement Theologies.

MODERN CONTROVERSIAL TEACHINGS

Today, Christians hold to a variety of teachings about God's Kingdom.

AMILLENNIALISM

The rise of Replacement Theology began in earnest in the second century and was enshrined as the major view among Christians after the time of Augustine in the early fifth century. It dominated the theology of Christendom for at least thirteen centuries. Its form was usually

Amillennialism, a term that means "no Millennium." However, this designation is somewhat misleading. Proponents of Amillennialism believe the thousand years in Revelation 20 describe the indefinite time between the First and Second Advents of Christ. What they deny is that the Millennium is a future, earthly Kingdom that begins when Jesus returns. In this scheme, the church in the present age is the Kingdom of God. This view is held by an overwhelming majority of Roman Catholics. Among Protestants, many adherents of Covenant Theology hold to it as do the proponents of the recent Progressive Covenantalism.

One of the major problems with this view is that the Second Coming recorded in Revelation 19 precedes the thousand years of chapter 20. This order seems to support Premillennialism, not Amillennialism. The frequently used amillennial answer down through the years has been its recapitulation view of the book of Revelation. This approach sees the book divided into seven sections (1—3; 4—7; 8—11; 12—14; 15—16; 17—19; and 20—22). Each section goes back over (recapitulates) the present age with various descriptions of what is transpiring, usually with an emphasis on the conflict between evil and believers.[3] Interestingly, a break is placed between chapters 19 and 20, so chapter 20 begins a new section that describes the events starting with the First Advent. Hence, the thousand years is about the present age.

Several difficulties prevent this recapitulation view from being acceptable. First, the sevenfold division of the book does not follow the threefold outline of Revelation given in the text itself in Revelation 1:19: "Write the things which you have seen, and the things which are, and the things which will take place after this." These three parts of Revelation correspond to most of chapter 1, chapters 2—3, and chapters 4—22.

Second, the word *and* occurs in the book more than 1,100 times. This usage reflects an ancient way of promoting consecutive narrative. As a result, it is hard to remove the chronology between chapters 19 and 20.

Third, there is a unity in the content of chapters 19 and 20 that cannot easily be dismissed. Chapter 19 reveals the destruction of the Beast (Antichrist) and False Prophet. Chapter 20 reveals the final end of Satan. The description of God's judgment of the unholy trinity goes together and should not be separated.

Fourth, there is the theological problem of the binding of Satan cited in Revelation 20:1–3. The recapitulation view teaches that the devil is bound in the present age. Sometimes proponents say Satan is active in attacking Christians today (Eph. 6:16; 1 Pet. 5:8), but the devil is not deceiving the unsaved among the nations.[4] However, the Bible teaches that Satan is highly active in blinding the minds of unbelievers at the present time (2 Cor. 4:3–4). In short, the recapitulation view of the book of Revelation makes no sense when all biblical truth is considered.

When the sixteenth-century Protestant Reformation arrived, leaders Martin Luther and John Calvin remained committed to Amillennialism. However, there was a return to more interest in literal, historical-grammatical interpretation in general. Christians began to read the Bible once again in a more straightforward way. As a result, the new view of Postmillennialism developed, and the biblical view of Premillennialism resurged.

POSTMILLENNIALISM

Postmillennialism is the view that the Second Coming of Christ occurs after the Millennium of Revelation 20. While not a biblical view, it does take the details of prophecy more seriously than Amillennialism. This viewpoint began to be popular after Daniel Whitby wrote his treatise on the Millennium in 1703. Jonathan Edwards, who died 1758, popularized this view for American Christians to the point that, throughout the 1800s, the postmillennial position on the Kingdom dominated evangelicalism in America.

The basic thrust of this view is that the church will eventually succeed in evangelizing a large part of the world's population, thereby Christianizing a majority of the world's institutions. In this way, the church will usher in an earthly Kingdom while Jesus is still in heaven. The more specific outline of Postmillennialism consists of the following: (1) The Papacy will eventually fall, (2) the Jewish people will then turn to Christ, (3) the Kingdom will begin, and (4) Christ will return at the end of the earthly Kingdom.

Although Whitby held to a literal thousand years, many postmillennialists today hold that the thousand years refer symbolically to an indefinite period of time, like amillennialists do. Such an approach is an overly optimistic view of the church triumphant. A more recent version of Postmillennialism, called Christian Reconstructionism, emerged in the middle of the twentieth century. Adherents believe Christians eventually will reconstruct society along Christian lines to usher in the Kingdom. This view is sometimes called Dominionism due to its strongly worded understanding of believers exercising dominion, even politically, in the development of the Kingdom. One could fairly call this view Postmillennialism on steroids.

Historical reality does not seem to support Postmillennialism. The Bible predicts war and decline in the end times (Dan. 7; 11; Mt. 24; Rev. 6—19), not a utopia or golden age brought in by the church. Postmillennialism does not fit the biblical teaching of Messiah Jesus returning personally to set up His Kingdom on Earth (Rev. 19—20). Few evangelicals today hold to this view, which began to decline in the twentieth century after two world wars and the Holocaust. The world does not seem to be getting better and better.[5]

PREMILLENNIALISM

Although Premillennialism never went off the scene throughout church history, a resurgence of this position took place after the Reformation. At the present time among American Bible-believing Christians, Premillennialism is the prevalent view on the Kingdom. All premillennialists hold that Jesus is coming back personally to set up His earthly Kingdom.

However, not all premillennial positions are identical in the details. One brand is called Historic Premillennialism.[6] The name of this view comes from the fact that the adherents believe it hearkens back to the historical position of the early church. Although there are variations, most historic premillennialists hold to these distinctives: posttribulation Rapture of the church, downplaying of the future for national Israel, and the church as the new Israel. This position is contrary to dispensational Premillennialism, which generally holds to a pretribulation Rapture of the church, a future for national Israel in its land, and a distinction between Israel and the church in God's plan and program for history.

A literal, grammatical-historical interpretation of the Bible undergirds the dispensational outlook on these issues.[7] The pretribulation Rapture can be supported by Christians' exemption from the Day of the Lord taught in 1 Thessalonians 4:13—5:9 and the time of worldwide testing cited in Revelation 3:10.

Perhaps the place where the literal understanding of Scripture comes out the strongest is in reading the Old Testament promises concerning the future of Israel. For example, the prophet Daniel taught that in the end-times days, the Messianic Son of Man will come to establish an earthly Kingdom in the last days at the time of the destruction of the little horn, or Antichrist (Dan. 7:7–14). Isaiah described a picture of the Messiah in Israel during His earthly Kingdom (Isa. 11).

Amos predicted a time when Israel would be in the land never to be uprooted again (Amos 9:11–15). Ezekiel looked ahead to a time when Israel will be restored physically and spiritually in its land with a future Temple (Ezek. 36—48). Zechariah portrayed the Lord returning to deliver Israel and Jerusalem in the last days (Zech. 12—14). Many other passages could be added to this list. Such promises are not an occasional side issue in the Old Testament text but are close to the heart of God's plan. God is not done with Israel in His blueprint for history.

However, this plan differs from God's design for the church. The church has no land. It is the international and spiritual body of Christ, not a political nation (Eph. 2—3). While Israel and the church share God, Christ, individual salvation, and the future Kingdom, there are many differences between the two as God sovereignly works out His will in the world. Dispensational Premillennialism does a good job of highlighting these truths from Scripture as we await the coming of Christ to establish His Kingdom on Earth.

ALREADY/NOT YET

Another popular view today is that the Messianic Kingdom is both now and in the future. This approach is expressed as "already/not yet." The already part is the present time; the not yet is when Jesus returns and consummates the Kingdom. Some versions of this view see the not-yet part of the Messianic Kingdom as the coming Millennium (progressive dispensationalists). Other proponents see the consummation of the Kingdom as the eternal state (amillennialists). Other adherents see a future for national Israel (progressive dispensationalists).

One implication of this view is that we are already living in the Messianic Kingdom today. Usually, this means that Jesus is sitting on the throne of David at the right hand of the Father in heaven at the present time. This view does not represent the best interpretation of Scripture. While Jesus certainly is the Messianic King, He is a King in waiting, not a King who is currently reigning in fulfillment of the Kingdom promises of the Old Testament (Heb. 1:1—2:5). It is the "world to come" in which Jesus reigns in fulfillment of promises for the Messianic Kingdom (Heb. 2:5).

Paul placed the Kingdom of Christ in the future (2 Tim. 4:1). This statement is given in the context of an exhortation to Timothy to preach the Word (v. 2). If Jesus were on David's throne today and we are already in the Messianic Kingdom, why would those truths not be invoked to exhort young Timothy? The rule of Christ in the hearts of believers today and as Head of the church in the present dispensation (Eph. 1:22–23) should not be viewed as phase one of the fulfillment of the promises concerning Israel and Messiah's coming Kingdom. Just as king David was anointed to be king long before he reigned, Messiah Jesus sits on a throne in heaven today as the anointed Christ but is not yet reigning as the King of Israel.

KINGDOM NOW THEOLOGY

Kingdom Now Theology, found in some charismatic circles, affirms a dominion spirit similar to but not identical to that found in Christian Reconstructionism. Proponents are not necessarily postmillennial. But they often believe Christians today must take dominion over culture, so Jesus will return, usually to establish His Kingdom. The means by which this event takes place varies but usually involves the use of the supernatural sign-gifts and extrabiblical revelation given to new apostles and prophets who lead the movement. Hoping to overcome the culture, they desire to Christianize society in preparation for the Lord's return. Thus, they are in the process of instituting the Kingdom now, at the present time.

The greatest problem with such a view is that nowhere does the Bible teach Christians to prepare for the coming of the Lord by conquering society.

SOCIAL GOSPEL

In the early 1900s, a great controversy erupted over the advancement of the social gospel. Liberalism promoted it while fundamental Christians preached the gospel of eternal life. The former was designed to save society; the latter was intended to save souls. The former was a kind of institution of the Kingdom on Earth as humanity marches forth. Unfortunately, a reappearance of elements of the social gospel under the guise of social-justice issues can be seen especially in the younger generation of Bible-believing Christians today.

To be sure, they should be supported to some degree. Organizations like The Friends of Israel (FOI) pay for the building of bomb shelters for Israel. FOI uses relief funds to help Jewish people in need all around the world. There is, however, no Kingdom view associated with these actions. All people in the world are made in God's image and are worth pursuing at all levels of life (Gen. 9:6; 1 Cor. 11:7; Jas. 3:9). Since the love ethic is taught in the Bible for all dispensations, Christians can and should show their love for others in meeting special needs (Mt. 25:35–40).

However, social actions such as these should not rise to the same level of importance as the gospel of eternal life. People need the Lord. Sin crushes society on every side. It is an individual problem, not only a social problem. Individuals need to see themselves as sinners separated from God (Rom. 3:10–23; 6:23; Eph. 2:1–3). They need to put their full trust in Christ alone for the forgiveness of sin (Jn. 3:1–16; Rom. 4:1–5; 10:9–13).

Good deeds, no matter how well intentioned, do not save a soul and give a home in heaven. A focus on political and social agendas cannot accomplish the needed individual results. Instead, the gospel of eternal life must be preached, so men and women can come to saving faith. The entire world needs to hear that Jesus died for our sins on the cross as our substitute (Isa. 53; 2 Cor. 5:21) and was raised from the dead for our justification (Rom. 4:25). The primary function of the church is to proclaim the gospel of eternal life and teach the whole counsel of God (Mt. 28:19–20), and this function should not be replaced by social-justice issues.

In today's focus on social justice, one particular issue often is overlooked. The greatest social-justice concern is really anti-Semitism. Yet liberal, liberation theologians, who are Marxist in orientation, have joined with Arab Muslims to attack Israel as the colonial oppressor of the Palestinian Arabs.[8] The constant harassment of Israel by the United Nations and much of the world today should be an embarrassment to people who know the history of the persecution of the Jewish people over the past several centuries.

However, such treatment of the Jewish people—and national Israel—does not surprise people who know the Bible. Serious trouble and persecution for the Jewish people is predicted for end-times days (Jer. 30:5–7; Rev. 12). The premillennial coming of Christ to set up His Kingdom on Earth will do away with the world's social wrongs. His coming also will provide a home in His Kingdom for people who have been saved through faith in His work on their behalf.

CONCLUSION

Excitement about God's Kingdom is natural. However, the interpreter must rightly divide God's Word. God rules in general sovereignty over all things in every age. Christ rules as Head of the church at the present time. Both of these truths are special in their own right. We have a big God who rules universally; nothing escapes His attention. Christians can take great heart in knowing that God is in charge and Jesus has a precious relationship with His church. We are one body with Him. Christ is in us; we are in Christ. No other religion has the Savior we possess.

But the most-exciting expression of God's work in the world is coming when Jesus returns to set up His earthly Kingdom. When He comes, He will come to Jerusalem where His throne will be located. Jews and Gentiles, Israel and the church, and everyone who knows Him will enjoy the ultimate blessing of God's earthly Kingdom. Arno Gaebelein, an associate editor of the original Scofield Reference Bible, framed this understanding of God's coming Kingdom in words that blow the trumpet even still:

> *What we mean, the only answer, the completest and never-failing answer to all our questions, is*
>
> **The Glorious Reappearing of the Lord Jesus Christ.**
>
> *This future event will answer every question, solve every problem which humanity faces today, and all the existing chaotic conditions, and bring about that golden age of which heathen poets dreamed, which the Bible promises is in store for the earth.*[9]

This statement is the biblical understanding of the Messianic Kingdom. May God hit the fast-forward button to get us there! Even so, come Lord Jesus.

CHAPTER FOURTEEN

God's Millennial Kingdom

Richard Schmidt

Whether you get your news from printed or online newspapers, radio programs, TV newscasts, or internet sites, negative stories tend to outweigh positive ones. Violence and murder grab headlines since editors and programmers are quick to follow the news adage, "If it bleeds, it leads."

These kinds of events are not new, however. The world has been in various states of chaos and violence since the fall of man recorded in Genesis 3. Adam and Eve's rebellion against God resulted in God's pronouncement of judgment on humans, the animal kingdom, and the physical earth (vv. 13–19). This decree resulted in mankind's spiritual death, which led to hatred and violence (4:5–8).

The Jewish people are no exception to experiencing hatred and severe persecution. Ever since the children of Israel left Canaan on their journey to Egypt, they have endured multiple dispersions from their land; anti-Semitic hatred; and murder through the pogroms, holocaust, terrorism, and individual attacks.

The Scriptures speak of a yet-future time of God's blessing on Earth, known theologically as the Millennial Kingdom. At that time, God will remove much of the curse He implemented at man's fall. Jesus Christ will reign from Jerusalem for a 1,000-year period after His Second Coming (Rev. 19:11–21; 20:1–6). (See chapter 13, "Controversial Teachings on the Kingdom," for a summary of the main interpretations of the Millennium that Christians hold.)

This future, literal, theocratic Kingdom will be headquartered in Jerusalem, where all true believers in the Lord from all of history will dwell. Old Testament saints, Church-Age Christians, and Tribulation saints will dwell with the Lord Jesus in their glorified bodies (Dan. 12:1–2; Rev. 20:4–5). In addition, individuals who survive the literal, seven-year Tribulation (Rev. 6—19) and are believers in the Lord Jesus Christ will enter the Millennium in natural bodies and will repopulate the earth (Mt. 25:1–13, 31–46).

Jesus taught His disciples to look forward to the future Millennial Kingdom and to pray for its inauguration when God's will will be done on Earth as it is in heaven (6:10). He expects us to do the same.

As we focus on the Millennial Kingdom, we will examine the final preparations for it; the powerful, theocratic, coming Ruler; the productive and peaceful environment; and the punitive end to the millennium.

FINAL PREPARATIONS

A key to understanding Bible prophecy and the many events yet to be fulfilled is to establish a basic timeline of future events. Shortly after Jesus' death, burial, resurrection, and ascension, the current Church Age began, made up of Jewish and Gentile individuals who have accepted Jesus Christ as their Savior (1 Cor. 10:32; 12:27; 15:3–4; Eph. 3:1–7; Col. 1:24–29).

The next major event on God's prophetic calendar is the Rapture, or removal of all Christians from Earth. Raptured Christians will meet Jesus Christ in the air; be given eternal, glorified bodies; and spend eternity with the Lord (1 Cor. 15:50–54; 1 Th. 4:13–18). After that, the Antichrist will confirm a covenant or peace treaty with Israel for seven years, known as the Tribulation, or Daniel's 70th week (Dan. 9:27; Mt. 24:21; Rev. 5—19). At the end of the Tribulation, the Lord Jesus Christ will return to Earth with the glorified saints. He will then kill His enemies gathered at Armageddon in Israel (Rev. 14:17–20; 16:16; 19:11–21).

The final sequence of events involves preparations for Jesus Christ to take His rightful place as the theocratic Ruler in His Millennial Kingdom. The world will return to a near Edenic condition where the effects of the fall are minimalized and rebellion against God is curtailed.

BINDING OF SATAN

The apostle John provided a short but powerful narrative on the

Millennium in Revelation 20:1–10. He stated six times in the first seven verses that the time period is 1,000 years, or a millennium. God will remove Satan from the Earth and lock him in "the bottomless pit" until the Millennium ends (vv. 1–3). Then God will let him loose and gather all individuals born during that time and who refused to accept the Lord Jesus Christ as the King of their lives. The rebellious masses will be "devoured by fire," and Satan will be cast into the lake of fire for eternity (vv. 7–10).

RESURRECTION OF THE SAINTS

Next is the "first resurrection." This term has caused theological debate since multiple people were resurrected in the past, and the Lord will resurrect the Church Age saints before it happens.

Multiple people were resurrected from the dead. The Old Testament recorded Elijah resurrecting the widow of Zarephath's son (1 Ki. 17:17–24) and the son of a Shunammite woman (2 Ki. 4:20–37). God's Spirit raised a dead man tossed into Elisha's tomb (13:21). The New Testament recorded Jesus raising the widow of Nain's son (Lk. 7:11–16), Jairus's 12-year-old daughter (Mk. 5:35–43), and Lazarus (Jn. 11:1–44). Peter raised Tabitha (Acts 9:36–41), and Paul raised Eutychus from the dead (20:7–12). Plus God resurrected multiple dead people when Jesus was crucified (Mt. 27:51–53). None of these individuals are included in the first resurrection since each of them experienced death a second time, and their physical bodies remain buried until the first resurrection.

The Bible clearly states that Jesus Christ was crucified, physically died, and was buried (1 Cor. 15:3–4). The most important event in history is the Lord Jesus Christ's resurrection from the dead (15:13–20). However, His resurrection was the firstfruits of the resurrection, and He is not included by definition in the future first resurrection.

Church Age believers, who are not part of the Jewish prophetic calendar (Dan. 9:24–27), comprise a unique group of God's people who will receive their resurrected, glorified bodies before the first resurrection of Revelation 20 (1 Cor. 15:50–54; 1 Th. 4:13–18). The Church Age was kept a mystery until revealed and developed in the book of Acts (Rom. 16:25–26; Eph. 3:1–7; Col. 1:24–29).

The first resurrection is specific to those who trusted in the Lord during the Old Testament and Tribulation periods (Dan. 12:1–2; 9:27). Both groups are part of God's prophetic calendar.[1]

REGATHERING OF THE JEWISH PEOPLE TO ISRAEL

Multiple prophetic passages in the Bible discuss the regathering of the Jewish people to Israel at the beginning of the Millennium. In summary, at the midpoint of the seven-year Tribulation, the Jewish people will suffer horrific persecution and flee from Jerusalem to the wilderness, where God will protect one third of them (Zech. 13:8–9; Mt. 24:16).

When Jesus returns to Earth at His Second Coming, He will gather the remnant of the Jewish people. They will experience a national conversion (Isa. 59:20–21; 65:7–19; Ezek. 11:17–20; Joel 2:28–32; Zech. 3:1–7; Rom. 11:26–27), and He will bring them to Jerusalem to serve Him in natural bodies (Dt. 30:1–5; Isa. 11:11–12; 65:9–10; Jer. 23:3; Ezek. 37:21–22; Micah 2:12; 4:6–7; Zeph. 2:6–7).

JUDGMENT OF THE NATIONS

God will judge the Gentile nations that survive the Tribulation period. A group of righteous Gentiles will enter the Millennial Kingdom in human bodies, and the unrighteous will be cast into everlasting fire. Jesus addressed this prophetic issue with His disciples in the Olivet Discourse (Mt. 25:31–46; cf. chap. 11, "The Kingdom in the Olivet Discourse"). God will command all Gentile nations who enter His Kingdom to attend the annual Feast of Tabernacles in Jerusalem or be judged with drought in their land (Zech. 14:16–17).

POWERFUL, THEOCRATIC RULER

Untold numbers of Christmas pageants quote Isaiah 9:6–7, suggesting that the baby Jesus came at His First Advent as the "Wonderful, Counselor, Mighty God, Everlasting Father, Prince of Peace." Nothing could be further from the truth. The Lord Jesus did come to Earth, as the first sentence in that passage states, "For unto us a Child is born, unto us a Son is given." He offered the Kingdom, but He was rejected and crucified.

The remainder of these two verses will be fulfilled at the Lord's Second Advent: "And the government will be upon His shoulder. And His name will be called Wonderful, Counselor, Mighty God, Everlasting

Father, Prince of Peace. Of the increase of His government and peace there will be no end, upon the throne of David and over His kingdom, to order it and establish it with judgment and justice from that time forward, even forever."

The powerful, theocratic ruler, the Lord Jesus Christ, will rule over the nations (Ps. 22:28–29). He will judge the people righteously and govern all the nations on Earth (Ps. 67:4). Some individuals born during the Millennium will not follow the King of kings, and the Lord will rule them with a rod of iron and slay the wicked (Ps. 2:9; Isa. 11:3–4; Rev. 2:27; 12:5).

When Christ returns to Earth to rule, three categories of resurrected saints in glorified bodies will accompany Him (Rev. 19:11–21). The first two include Old Testament saints (Dan. 12:2) and martyred Tribulation saints (Rev. 6:9–11; 20:4–6). God will resurrect these individuals at the future first resurrection.[2] Raptured Church Age saints comprise the final group that will rule and reign with the Lord Jesus (1 Cor. 15:51–54; 1 Th. 4:13–18; 2 Tim. 2:12).[3]

The first resurrection is the final resurrection of the righteous. No person who is a true believer in Christ will die during the Millennial Kingdom. Therefore, individuals born then and who receive Jesus Christ as their Savior will never experience physical death.[4]

PRODUCTIVE AND PEACEFUL ENVIRONMENT

When the Lord Jesus Christ takes His rightful place as the theocratic ruler in the Millennial Kingdom, numerous positive changes will affect humans, animals, and the earth. God's Kingdom will exemplify the best conditions on Earth since the Garden of Eden before the fall of man. People born during that Kingdom will possess a sin nature, which requires each person to trust the Lord Jesus as Savior or suffer potential early death and guaranteed eternal judgment.[5]

LONGEVITY OF LIFE

One positive change is how long people will live. When Jesus Christ takes His throne in Jerusalem at the beginning of the Millennium, He will welcome into His Kingdom an unknown number of Jewish and Gentile believers who survived the Tribulation period (Mt. 25:1–13, 31–46). Longevity of life returns back to the days of Genesis when people lived longer than 900 years (Gen. 5:5–20). Methuselah, the longest living person in the Bible, died at 969 years of age (v. 27). Therefore, God can easily sustain the life of the righteous during the entire Millennial Kingdom.

Zechariah expanded on the length of life during the Kingdom Age when he stated, "Thus says the Lord of hosts: 'Old men and old women shall again sit in the streets of Jerusalem, each one with his staff in his hand because of great age'" (Zech. 8:4). Great age will include people living hundreds of years as they enjoy the blessings of long life.

Isaiah wrote, "No more shall an infant from there live but a few days, nor an old man who has not fulfilled his days; for the child shall die one hundred years old, but the sinner being one hundred years old shall be accursed" (Isa. 65:20). Millions of people will be born then. Anyone who dies during the Millennium does so because of his or her abhorrent behavior and rejection of the Messiah. Despite the fact that the Lord Jesus Christ is ruling from Jerusalem, as many as "the sand of the sea" will reject Him (Rev. 20:7–9).

PEACE

A second positive change is peace. Since the fall of man in the Garden of Eden, the world has experienced continual hatred, violence, and wars. Christ's theocratic Kingdom will experience a world without conflicts and wars. Micah the prophet stated the Messiah "shall judge between many peoples, and rebuke strong nations afar off; they shall beat their swords into plowshares, and their spears into pruning hooks; nation shall not lift up sword against nation, neither shall they learn war anymore" (Mic. 4:3). Isaiah reiterated the same message, based on the fact that the Lord Jesus will reign from Jerusalem and teach all people His ways (Isa. 2:2–4). Zechariah prophesied that the people who dwell in Jerusalem will no longer face utter destruction, but the city shall be inhabited safely (Zech. 14:11).

The prophetic Scriptures speak to the change in the animal kingdom, where former flesh-eating beasts will graze in the fields in harmony. Children will play with venomous snakes and not be bitten. A child will encounter a lion, bear, or other former ferocious beast, and the two will walk together without a violent encounter (Isa. 11:6–9; 65:23–25). The curse the animal kingdom experienced at the fall of man will be lifted.

LAND AND SEA CHANGES

Another positive change in the Millennium Kingdom is seen in agriculture. Recent travelers to Israel report significant changes in the growth of agriculture in desert areas in many parts of the country. I have personally driven through deserts in Israel. In the midst of the brown, sun-burned land, a large, beautiful grove of well-maintained date palm trees were growing. These recent developments point to the prophetic future when the entire land of Israel will experience a change, turning it from an unproductive desert to a land filled with blossoming agricultural products (35:1–2).

Isaiah wrote about the safe and productive land. The Jewish people will "build houses and inhabit them; they shall plant vineyards and eat their fruit. They shall not build and another inhabit; they shall not plant and another eat; for as the days of a tree, so shall be the days of My people, and My elect shall long enjoy the work of their hands" (65:21–22). The Lord's Kingdom will experience productivity in the land that was unheard of in past generations.

The Dead Sea is the lowest place on earth, registering nearly 1,400 feet below sea level on the surface. It cannot sustain any fish or animal life. People who venture into the water must keep their heads above it or suffer horrific burning in their eyes and mucus membranes. The water ruins the frames and motors of boats; therefore, only a few custom-made government boats ever venture into it.

Ezekiel revealed that during the Millennium, God will transform the Dead Sea into living waters. He will form a river that flows from underneath the Temple in Jerusalem toward the Dead Sea. The miraculous change occurs when "this water flows toward the eastern region, goes down into the valley, and enters the sea. When it reaches the sea, its waters are healed. And it shall be that every living thing that moves, wherever the rivers go, will live. There will be a very great multitude of fish, because these waters go there; for they will be healed, and everything will live wherever the river goes" (Ezek. 47:8–9).

WORSHIP

Perhaps the most significant change in the Millennium is worship of the Lord Jesus Christ. He will reign from His Temple in Jerusalem (Zech. 6:12–13). The King of kings and Lord of lords will dwell with the believers of all ages and those in physical bodies for the entire 1,000 years. Because Jesus is God, the Creator and Sustainer of all things (Col. 1:16), it should go without saying that He is most worthy of worship. To support this worship, the land will experience a massive change at the beginning of the Millennium as recorded in Ezekiel 40—48. Randall Price summarized it this way: "The millennial city of Jerusalem and the Temple will together encompass a 2,500-square-mile area. The portion reserved for the priests and Levites is some 50 miles, while the Temple courts will be one mile square. These dimensions are larger than those of the modern State of Israel."[6]

The Lord will reinstate the sacrificial system (Isa. 56:6–7; 66:20–21; Jer. 33:18; Ezek. 40—48; Zech. 14:16–21). Price provided a scholarly argument that the Millennial sacrifices will allow the nations to maintain a status of ceremonial purity: "Sacrificial 'atonement' is not for salvation, nor for inward sanctification, but to preserve outward corporate 'sanctification' (or ceremonial purification) so that a holy God can remain in the midst of an unholy people."[7] The Millennium, in contrast to the Church Age, will incorporate the sacrificial system to ceremonially cleanse, or purify the nations, which include the millions of people born with a sin nature during the 1,000 years.[8]

The Scriptures are replete with the concept of the masses worshiping the Lord during His kingdom. For example, "All the ends of the world shall remember and turn to the LORD, and all the families of the nations shall worship before You" (Ps. 22:27). Micah wrote,

> *Many nations shall come and say, "Come, and let us go up to the mountain of the LORD, to the house of the God of Jacob; He will teach us His ways, and we shall walk in His paths." For out of Zion the law shall go forth, and the word of the LORD from Jerusalem. He shall judge between many peoples, and rebuke strong nations afar off; they shall beat their swords into plowshares, and their spears into pruning hooks; nation shall not lift up sword against nation, neither shall they learn war anymore* (Mic. 4:2–3).

Christ's theocratic Millennial Kingdom will be as close to heaven on Earth as has ever existed since the Garden of Eden.

The prophet Zechariah made a startling statement to the people who will live during the Millennial Kingdom. God mandated through him that all nations must go to Jerusalem once a year to worship the King during the Feast of Tabernacles. God will judge with drought those who refuse to go and worship the Lord Jesus (Zech. 14:16–17).

PUNITIVE END

Despite Christ physically reigning on Earth during the Millennial Kingdom, many people born during that time will refuse to accept Jesus as their Lord and Savior. The apostle John revealed the process that God will use to rid His Kingdom of the unregenerate. At the end of the Millennium, Satan will be released from the bottomless pit (Rev. 20:7), getting one more chance to roam free on Earth in his attempt to stop God's plan. But he will fail once again.

Satan will rapidly move into the world where God will allow him to deceive the nations that refuse to worship the Lord Jesus. The devil will use his deceptive schemes to build hatred in the rebellious nations against God's people in Jerusalem. This anti-God rhetoric will gain the support of the unrighteous. Then this massive group, numbering as "the sand of the sea," will move toward Jerusalem with the goal of destroying God's people. Satan's hatred of God and His saints will be shared by the masses who surround the City of God for one final battle (Rev. 20:8).

The King of kings will meet the huge army of Satan's followers at Jerusalem with a consuming fire (v. 9). God will cast Satan into the lake of fire, where he will spend eternity in torture with the haters of God, including the Antichrist and the false prophet (19:20; 20:10). The Lord will then move into the final events that close out the present heavens and Earth and prepare the world for the new heaven and new earth (Is. 65:17; 66:22; 2 Pet. 3:13).

CONTEMPORARY CHALLENGE

We have a lot to look forward to! Knowing God's plans for the future should motivate us to spread the Good News of salvation from sin through faith in the Lord Jesus Christ and to live in such a way that we are ready for His coming and not ashamed to meet our Lord.

CHAPTER FIFTEEN

God's Eternal Kingdom on Earth

Bruce Scott

How do you begin to describe another world, a world that is remarkably different and unnatural from your own? Even though words may fail you, you still must attempt to use them to communicate what you know and what you see.

This was the challenge for the apostle John, who, when he wrote the book of Revelation, was not writing a fantasy novel but, rather, God-breathed Scripture. In chapters 21 and 22, John attempted to describe another world, another time and place in what theologians have termed the eternal state or the eternal Kingdom. In those chapters, John, through the ministry of the Holy Spirit, put into words that which "eye has not seen, nor ear heard, nor have entered into the heart of man the things which God has prepared for those who love Him" (1 Cor. 2:9).

The best word to describe this world is *new*—not only new in time, but new in kind. As God declared in Revelation 21:5, "Behold, I make all things new."

NEW CREATION OF THE ETERNAL KINGDOM

After Jesus returns at His Second Coming, God's Kingdom on Earth will initially last for one 1,000 years (20:6). Following Satan's final rebellion, the Great White Throne Judgment, and the casting of death and hades into the lake of fire (vv. 7–14), Christ's Kingdom will then be turned over to the Father to meld into His eternal Kingdom (1 Cor. 15:24–26).

The eternal Kingdom will begin with a new creation, the creation of a new heaven and earth: "Now I saw a new heaven and a new earth, for the first heaven and the first earth had passed away" (Rev. 21:1). Although the concept of a new heaven and earth is found only in a few passages of Scripture (Ps. 102:25–26; Isa. 65:17; 66:22; 2 Pet. 3:13), the future reality of it is sure.

The reason there will be a new heaven and earth is that the former ones will pass away, apparently at the time of the Great White Throne Judgment (Rev. 20:11). The apostle Peter described how the old heaven and Earth will pass away, dissolved by intense heat and fire (2 Pet. 3:7, 10–12).

This event should remind us that, apart from two things in this world—God's Word and human souls—everything we see today is going to be burned up in the end. Since that is the case, perhaps we should ask ourselves how much time, energy, and resources do we want to invest in temporal things instead of eternal things? As Peter reminded us, "Therefore, since all these things will be dissolved, what manner of persons ought you to be in holy conduct and godliness?" (v. 11).

What will the new heaven be like? We are not given much information. The Bible tells us that heaven is a created place (Gen. 1:1; Rev. 10:6; 14:7). The word *heaven* is used in three ways in the Scriptures: (1) to refer to the sky, where birds fly and from where rain falls (Gen. 1:20; Rev. 11:6); (2) to refer to space, where the sun, moon, and stars are located (Rev. 6:13; Gen. 1:16–17); and (3) to refer to the "heavens of heavens" (Ps. 148:4), "third heaven," or "Paradise" (2 Cor. 12:2, 4), the dwelling place of God, holy angels, and believers who have died. All of this will be made new in the eternal Kingdom.

A primary difference, though, between the new heaven and the current one is that the place where God, holy angels, and believers will be dwelling is on the new earth, not in the present third heaven. What will the new earth be like? Again, we are not told much. It apparently will be a sphere, as it is today, because we read in Revelation 21:13 that the points of the compass will be used to designate the twelve gates of New Jerusalem.

One thing we are told about the new earth is that there will be no sea (v. 1).

Today, land covers 29 percent of the Earth's surface, while water covers 71 percent. Of the latter, more than 96 percent is found in the oceans.[1] With the absence of seas, it appears that land will cover the majority of the new earth. One should not suppose, however, that the absence of seas in the eternal Kingdom also implies the absence of fresh water. We also know there will be at least one great and high mountain in the new earth (v. 10). Therefore, the terrain will not be one enormous, flat plain.

Furthermore, the curse on the earth will be lifted (22:3), reversing what happened to God's earthly Kingdom back in Genesis. There we read that because of man's sin, the ground was cursed and death entered the world (Gen. 3:17–18). Ever since, all creation has continually groaned, waiting for the day when the curse will be lifted (Rom. 8:19–22). What is amazing to ponder is that all of the stunning beauty and grandeur we currently see all around us in God's creation is a beauty and grandeur that has been cursed! It is not what God originally made or planned. It is a world under a terrible curse of distortion and corruption. But one day, that curse will be lifted; and there will be nothing preventing God's new earth from bursting forth in fullness of life. If this present, beautiful earth is under a curse, is it possible to even imagine what the new earth will look like?

How glorious will the new heaven and earth be? God declared in Isaiah 65:17, "For behold, I create new heavens and a new earth; and the former shall not be remembered or come to mind." In that day, we will not remember the Grand Canyon, Mount Everest, Niagara Falls, or any other magnificent scenery here on Earth. We will not recall their splendor, nor will we even want to do so. Such will be the glory and spectacle of the new heaven and new earth.

NEW CITY OF THE ETERNAL KINGDOM

In the eternal Kingdom, there will be a new city, the holy city, New Jerusalem: "Then I, John, saw the holy city, New Jerusalem, coming down out of heaven from God, prepared as a bride adorned for her husband" (Rev. 21:2). This will be an actual, literal, material city. It is not figurative, nor is it a metaphor for the church, even though its description uses marriage-type language (vv. 2, 9).

From where does the city originate? It comes down out of heaven from God (v. 2). It apparently was created at the same time the heavens were created because Paul spoke of "the Jerusalem above" in the present tense (Gal. 4:26), indicating it was in existence even in his time.

New Jerusalem will have a fascinating structure. On the outside, it is surrounded by a great and high wall, 144 cubits in height (Rev. 21:12, 17), or 216 feet. In comparison, the Great Wall of China is only twenty-five feet high in places. The wall surrounding the city will be almost nine times as high. The wall itself is built of jasper, a precious stone (v. 18). Supporting the wall are twelve foundation stones, each consisting of its own precious stone or gem (vv. 14, 19–20). Not all these stones can be identified with complete accuracy; but most interpreters agree that at least they will be of the purest quality, brilliant in their colors and shades of white, green, blue, red, purple, and yellow.

In each of the four walls are three gates that are never closed (vv. 12–13, 25). Each gate is made of one, single pearl, large enough for people to walk through. What is true about the highest quality of pearls is, of course, true of these in the eternal Kingdom: They are almost always iridescent, meaning they appear to display a variety of colors as in a rainbow, depending on the angle at which you view them. Imagine how beautiful these pearls will be, along with the foundation stones, when you consider the amount of light that will be reflecting off them!

Behind the walls, the new city itself will be amazing in size and beauty. The text says the city is laid out as a square (v. 16). But because its height is equal to its length and width, it is more in the shape of a cube. What are its dimensions? The New King James Version says 12,000 furlongs. The Greek says 12,000 stadia. A stadion was a unit of measuring distance, 600-625 feet long. Therefore, 12,000 stadia are equal to at least 7,200,000 feet, or almost 1,400 miles. So the length, width, and height of New Jerusalem will be about 1,400 miles.

These dimensions are difficult to grasp. Perhaps, by comparison, we might be able to comprehend how massive New Jerusalem will be. For example, most commercial airplanes fly at a cruising altitude of 33,000 feet or six and a quarter miles above Earth. This city will be 224 times higher than that. Technically, outer space is considered by international agreement to begin at sixty-two miles (100 km.) above mean sea level.[2] New Jerusalem will be twenty-three times higher than that. NASA space shuttles orbited the planet at about the same altitude as the International Space Station, around 200 miles above Earth.[3] New Jerusalem will be seven times higher than that. Finally, the National Oceanic and Atmospheric Administration has polar-orbiting satellites

540 miles up in the highest layer of Earth's atmosphere known as the exosphere.[4] New Jerusalem will be almost three times higher than that.

Now we know why Jesus said, "In my Father's house are many mansions" (Jn. 14:2).

Not only will the new city be impressive in its size, but also in its beauty. It will be as beautiful "as a bride adorned for her husband" (Rev. 21:2). The city and its street will be pure gold, like clear glass (vv. 18, 21).

NEW CITIZENS OF THE ETERNAL KINGDOM

Since the new city will be large in size and there also will be a new earth, who will inhabit them? The Bible tells us there will be many citizens of the eternal Kingdom. One group are angels, some of whom (and not Saint Peter) will guard or stand watch at the twelve pearly gates (21:12; Heb. 12:22).

Another group of citizens are resurrected believers from every age. Abraham will be there (Heb. 11:8–10), as well as other Old Testament believers (vv. 13–16). The believing remnant of Israel also will be there. Note that the twelve gates of the city wall have the names of the twelve tribes of Israel written on them (Rev. 21:12). These names indicate Israel will still be a distinct entity in God's Kingdom, fulfilling eternal covenants and promises God made to them. Every time someone walks through those gates and reads the name of one of the tribes of Israel, he or she will be reminded of John 4:22, "Salvation is of the Jews."

Also inhabiting the new city and the Kingdom will be the true church, the body of Christ (Heb. 12:22–23). Note that the twelve foundation stones of the city wall also have the names of the twelve apostles written on them (Rev. 21:14). Finally, believing Gentiles, who are not converts to Israel or part of the church, will be there as well (vv. 24, 26).

What is sobering is that entrance to the new city and the Kingdom is restricted and conditional. Only overcomers will inherit it (v. 7). "Who is he who overcomes the world, but he who believes that Jesus is the Son of God?" (1 Jn. 5:5). Also, only people whose names are written in the Lamb's Book of Life may enter (Rev. 21:27).

People who cannot enter the city but, rather, are the inhabitants of the lake of fire, are described as "the cowardly, unbelieving, abominable, murderers, sexually immoral, sorcerers, idolaters, and all liars" (v. 8). But why are these people excluded from the city when many Christians have committed these same sins in their own backgrounds? By not believing in Christ, sadly, they died in their sins. They are not in Christ. Their names are, therefore, still in the book of death, rather than in the Lamb's Book of Life.

Finally, of course, the most important inhabitant of the new city and the eternal Kingdom will be God Himself (v. 3).

NEW CIVILIZATION OF THE ETERNAL KINGDOM

The eternal Kingdom will also have new living conditions, a new civilization. For example, there will be a new theocratic government. The kings and nations of the earth will bring their glory and honor into the holy city, demonstrating their total and utter submission to that government (vv. 24, 26). God and Jesus the Lamb will sit on the throne (22:1, 3). The Lamb will have servants who will see His face, have His name on their foreheads, and reign with Him forever and ever (2 Tim. 2:12; Rev. 22:3–5).

Although we won't need to eat and drink in the Kingdom, we can if we choose to do so since food and water will be available (Rev. 2:7, 17; 22:1–2). After all, Jesus ate while in His resurrected body (Lk. 24:41–43).

Much of what will make the eternal Kingdom new is the absence of certain conditions we experience now. For example, no one will die in the eternal Kingdom in contrast to nearly two people dying every second in this world.[5] No more funerals. No more wailing over the loss of a loved one. No more grieving over the loss of a child. None of these events will ever happen again. That is why there will be no more sorrow or mourning or crying. John euphemistically described the tenderness of our caring God when he wrote, "And God will wipe away every tear from their eyes" (Rev. 21:4).

No more pain will be another new condition in the Kingdom (v. 4). No more pain when you bang your finger with a hammer. No more bruised knees. No more stubbed toes. No more headaches. No more colds. No more flu. No more allergies. No more arthritis. No more kidney stones. No more heart attacks. No more cancer.

And not only will there be no more physical pain, but emotional pain will be gone, as well. No more disappointments. No more depression. No more humiliation. No more rejection. No more isolation. No more loneliness. No more tragedies. No more broken hearts.

Why won't any of these conditions be present? Because there will be no more sin. When sin entered the world, death did, too, through sin (Rom. 5:12). But all of that will be gone in God's Kingdom.

Also lacking in the new city is a temple "for the Lord God Almighty and the Lamb are its temple" (Rev. 21:22).

New Jerusalem will have no need of the sun, moon, or a lamp (v. 23; 22:5). Notice the text does not say there will be no sun or moon, only that there will be no need of them for illumination. However, the sun and moon may be needed for keeping time (Gen. 1:14: Rev. 22:2). Living in the eternal Kingdom does not necessarily mean there will be no observance of time, since humans, unlike God, are finite beings who live within and not outside of time and space. In the Kingdom, though, time will have no end. Another purpose of the sun and moon might be to serve as a witness of God's eternal preservation of the nation of Israel (Jer. 31:35–36).

There also will be no night due to the absolute effulgence of light that will fill the city. It will, therefore, be daytime all of the time in the holy city, so much so that the nations shall walk in its light (Rev. 21:24–25; 22:5). From where does the light come? It comes from the glory of God shining out from the Lamb of God (21:11, 23; 22:5). Jesus Christ will be the lamp that contains God's glory, which will shine in all its radiance. He truly is "the brightness of His glory" (Heb. 1:3). As the apostle John said, "God is light and in Him is no darkness at all" (1 Jn. 1:5).

CLEAR CALLING OF THE ETERNAL KINGDOM

One more feature of the eternal Kingdom that has import even for the present time is the water of life, a fountain and river, clear as crystal (Rev. 21:6; 22:1). Notice four aspects of this water: (1) It is for people who are thirsty (v. 6; 22:17). (2) It comes directly from the throne of God and the Lamb (22:1). In other words, it is not man-made; it is sourced only in God. (3) It is free. You may drink without cost (21:6; 22:17). (4) You are invited, not forced, to drink from it (v. 17).

This water of life in the eternal Kingdom is symbolic of Jesus Christ and the salvation He offers to every thirsty soul. On one occasion, "Jesus stood and cried out, saying, 'If anyone thirsts, let him come to Me and drink'" (Jn. 7:37). The citizens in the future Kingdom will be there because they have accepted Jesus' invitation in this present life.

Will you be one of those people? Is your soul thirsty? Thirsty for truth? Thirsty for cleansing from guilt and sin? Thirsty for overcoming? Thirsty for an eternal relationship with God?

If so, then I urge you to put your faith, your trust, in Jesus Christ alone, the Lamb of God who took away the sin of the world. Believe in your heart that He died to pay for your sins and rose from the dead to give you the free gift of eternal life. Believe, and your name will be written in the Lamb's book of life.

"And the Spirit and the bride say, 'Come!' And let him who hears say, 'Come!' And let him who thirsts come. Whoever desires, let him take the water of life freely" (Rev. 22:17).

Will you come to Jesus and quench your thirst?

SURE COMING OF THE ETERNAL KINGDOM

Christians are sometimes accused of being disconnected from reality, as if all we live for is some sort of "pie in the sky." But that charge is not true. We live for Jesus Christ (2 Cor. 5:15).

At the same time, waiting and looking forward to our heavenly inheritance is nothing to be ashamed of. It is promised (1 Pet. 1:3–4). Our citizenship is not here on this earth (Phil. 3:20). Our citizenship is sourced in heaven, in New Jerusalem, which will come to the new earth in the eternal Kingdom.

When that event occurs, what Jesus said in His model prayer will finally come to pass: "Your kingdom come. Your will be done on earth as it is in heaven" (Mt. 6:10).

"Surely I am coming quickly," said Jesus. And we echo John's response, "Amen. Even so, come, Lord Jesus!" (Rev. 22:20).

ENDNOTES

CHAPTER TWO

[1] Alva J. McClain, *The Greatness of the Kingdom* (Winona Lake, IN: BMH Books, 1974), 26.
[2] Many texts teach the triune God; Isaiah 48:16 and Matthew 28:19 are two of them.
[3] John F. Walvoord, *Prophecy Knowledge Handbook* (Wheaton, IL: Victor Books, 1991), 20.
[4] J. Vernon McGee, *Thru the Bible with J. Vernon McGee* (Nashville, TN: Thomas Nelson, 1981), 23.
[5] Arnold G. Fruchtenbaum, *Messianic Christology: A Study of Old Testament Prophecy Concerning the First Coming of the Messiah* (Tustin, CA: Ariel Ministries, 1998), 14.
[6] Michael J. Vlach, *He Will Reign Forever: A Biblical Theology of the Kingdom* (Silverton, OR: Lampion Press, 2017), 69.
[7] Walter C. Kaiser Jr., *The Messiah in the Old Testament* (Grand Rapids, MI: Zondervan Publishing House, 1995), 42.
[8] Fruchtenbaum, 15.

CHAPTER THREE

[1] H. C. Leupold, "326 גוה" in *Theological Wordbook of the Old Testament*, eds. R. Laird Harris, Gleason L. Archer Jr., and Bruce K. Waltke (Chicago: Moody Press, 1980), 154.
[2] James Montgomery Boice, *Genesis: An Expositional Commentary*, vol. 2 (Grand Rapids, MI: Baker Books, 1998), 562.
[3] H. C. Leupold, *Exposition of Genesis* (Grand Rapids, MI: Baker Book House, 1942), 488.
[4] Leupold, 488–489.
[5] John F. Walvoord, "The Abrahamic Covenant and Premillennialism," *Bibliotheca Sacra* 109, (January, 1952) no. 433, 38-40.
[6] J. Dwight Pentecost, *Thy Kingdom Come* (Grand Rapids, MI: Kregel Publications, 1995), 62.

CHAPTER FOUR

1. Ed Hindson and Thomas Ice, *Charting the Bible Chronologically* (Eugene, OR: Harvest House Publishers, 2016), 57.
2. Alva J. McClain, *The Greatness of the Kingdom* (Winona Lake, IN: BMH Books, 1959), 53-58.
3. Walter C. Kaiser Jr., "Exodus," *The Expositor's Bible Commentary: Genesis, Exodus, Leviticus, Numbers*, vol. 2, ed. Frank E. Gaebelein (Grand Rapids, MI: Zondervan Publishing House, 1990), 415.
4. Andrew M. Woods, *The Coming Kingdom: What Is the Kingdom and How Is Kingdom Now Theology Changing the Focus of the Church?* (Duluth, MN: Grace Gospel Press, 2016), 24.
5. McClain, 62.
6. McClain, 63.
7. "Judaism: The 613 Mitzvot (Commandments)," Jewish Virtual Library, www.jewishvirtuallibrary.org/the-613-mitzvot-commandments-2.
8. Leon Wood, *A Survey of Israel's History* (Grand Rapids, MI: Zondervan Publishing House, 1970), 148.
9. Kaiser, 420.
10. Francis Brown, with the cooperation of S. R. Driver and Charles A. Briggs, *The Brown-Driver-Briggs Hebrew and English Lexicon* (Peabody, MA: Hendrickson Publishing, 1906), 497-499.
11. McClain, 65.
12. Kaiser, 429-440.
13. Kaiser, 442.
14. Kaiser, 443-445.
15. J. Dwight Pentecost, *Thy Kingdom Come* (Grand Rapids, MI: Kregel Publications, 1995), 87-92.
16. Pentecost, 94.
17. Michael J. Vlach, *He Will Reign Forever* (Silverton, OR: Lampion Press, 2017), 97.

CHAPTER SIX

1. For an example, see J. Randall Price, "Dead Sea Scrolls, Eschatology of the" in *Dictionary of Premillennial Theology*, ed. Mal Couch (Grand Rapids, MI: Kregel Publications, 1996), 89-91.
2. Some translations say "the kingdom of God is within you." To take these words to refer to something internal to an individual does not fit

the context. Rather, it is "within you" in the sense of "among you" or "in your midst."
3   G. I. Williamson, *The Westminster Confession of Faith for Study Classes*, 2nd ed. (Phillipsburg, NJ: P&R Publishing Company, 2004), 340.
4   Stanley D. Toussaint, *Behold the King* (Portland, OR: Multnomah, 1980), 156.
5   It is a historical fact that some first-century Jews in Israel saw the death of Messiah in the Old Testament. It is widely reported in scholarly literature today that some Jewish people taught there were two Messiahs, one to die and one to rule and reign. However, for the most part, the Jewish people tended to ignore or downplay the death passages.

CHAPTER SEVEN

1   Donald A. Hagner, *Matthew 1–13*, vol. 33A, Word Biblical Commentary (Grand Rapids, MI: Zondervan, 2000), 86.
2   Ulrich Luz, *Matthew 1–7: A Commentary*, rev. ed., vol. 61A in Hermeneia, trans. James E. Crouch (Minneapolis, MN: Fortress Press, 2007), 183.
3   Michael J. Vlach, *He Will Reign Forever: A Biblical Theology of the Kingdom of God* (Silverton, OR: Lampion Press, 2017), 302.
4   Vlach, 309.
5   R. T. France, *The Gospel of Matthew* in The New International Commentary on the New Testament (Grand Rapids: William B. Eerdmans, 2007), 168.
6   Vlach, 310.
7   Vlach, 300.

CHAPTER EIGHT

1   Flavius Josephus, *The Wars of the Jews*, 7.6.2.
2   Flavius Josephus, *The Antiquities of the Jews*, 18.5.2.
3   Walter Bauer, *A Greek–English Lexicon of the New Testament and Other Early Christian Literature*, 3rd ed., rev. and ed. by Frederick William Danker (Chicago: The University of Chicago Press, 2001), 173c.
4   Chapter Nine
5   Alexander Balmain Bruce, *The Parabolic Teaching of Christ: A Systematic and Critical Study of the Parables of Our Lord*, 3rd rev. ed. (New York: A.

C. Armstrong and Son, 1904), 42.

6. James Montgomery Boice, *The Gospel of Matthew*, vol. 1 (Grand Rapids, MI: Baker Books, 2001), 230.
7. Charles Caldwell Ryrie, *Ryrie Study Bible*, expanded ed., New American Standard Bible 1995 update (Chicago: Moody Press, 1995), 1584, n. 4:2.
8. Gerhard Kittel and Gerhard Friedrich, eds., *Theological Dictionary of the New Testament*, abridged in one vol. by Geoffrey W. Bromily (Grand Rapids, MI: William B. Eerdmans, 1985), 775.
9. Stanley D. Toussaint, *Behold the King* (Grand Rapids, MI: Kregel Publications, 1980), 169.
10. Toussaint, 171.
11. Toussaint, 176.
12. D. A. Carson, "Matthew" in *The Expositor's Bible Commentary: Matthew, Mark, Luke*, vol. 8, ed. Frank E. Gaebelein (Grand Rapids, MI: Zondervan Publishing House, 1984), 316–317.
13. Michael J. Vlach, *He Will Reign Forever: A Biblical Theology of the Kingdom of God* (Silverton, OR: Lampion Press, 2017), 331.

CHAPTER ELEVEN

1. Known as the Rambam, Maimonides was among the greatest Jewish scholars of all time.
2. "Hilchos Melachim" from *Mishneh Torah of the Rambam*, 11:1, quoted in "What Did the Rabbis Say?" jewishroots.net.
3. Randall Price, "Understanding the Olivet Discourse," *Israel My Glory*, May/June 2005, 13.
4. John, G. Butler, *Jesus Christ: His Parables* (Clinton, IA: LBC Publications, 2002), 17.
5. David, M. Levy, "What Did Jesus Mean...(Mt. 24:34)?" *Israel My Glory*, March/April 2018, 27.
6. David M. Levy, "The Day of Accountability (Matthew 25:1–46)," *Israel My Glory*, April/May 1994, 23.

CHAPTER TWELVE

1. John Calvin, *Calvin's Commentaries* (Complete), trans. John King (Edinburgh: Calvin Translation Society, 1847), Accordance Bible software.

[2] F. F. Bruce, *The Book of the Acts* (Grand Rapids, MI: William B. Eerdmans, 1988), 35–36.
[3] Darrell L. Bock, *Acts* (Grand Rapids, MI: Baker Academic, 2007), 176-177.
[4] *Shemot Rabbah*, 25:12
[5] Bock, 62.

CHAPTER THIRTEEN

[1] The word *chiliasm* comes from the Greek word for 1,000 (*chilia*), which occurs six times in Revelation 20:1-7.
[2] One must be careful not to accuse all individuals today who hold to Replacement Theology of being anti-Semitic. Anti-Semitism is only part of the historical development of this view.
[3] See Anthony A. Hoekema, "Amillennialism" in *The Meaning of the Millennium: Four Views*, ed. Robert G. Clouse (Downers Grove, IL: InterVarsity Press, 1977), 155-187 and Kim Riddlebarger, *A Case for Amillennialism: Understanding the End Times* (Grand Rapids, MI: Baker Books, 2003), 200-206.
[4] Sam Storms, *Kingdom Come: The Amillennial Alternative* (Scotland: Christian Focus Publications, 2013), 439-42.
[5] Shortly after World War II and the Holocaust and during the Communism Red Scare, Loraine Boettner wrote *The Millennium* (The Presbyterian and Reformed Publishing Company, 1957), a well-intentioned but overly optimistic book. One chapter is titled "The World is Growing Better."
[6] Craig L. Blomberg and Sung Wook Chung, eds. *A Case for Historic Premillennialism: An Alternative to "Left Behind" Eschatology* (Grand Rapids, MI: Baker Academic, 2009).
[7] Charles C. Ryrie, *Dispensationalism*, rev. and expanded (Chicago: Moody Press, 1995), 40, 79-95.
[8] Paul R. Wilkinson, *Israel Betrayed, Volume 2: The Rise of Christian Palestinianism* (San Antonio, TX: Ariel Ministries, 2018).
[9] Arno Clemens Gaebelein, *The Hope of the Ages* (New York: Publication Office of "Our Hope," 1938), 72.

CHAPTER FOURTEEN

[1] My book *Daniel's Gap Paul's Mystery* (Hales Corners, WI: Prophecy

Focus Ministries, 2016) covers the distinctiveness of Church-Age saints in contrast to Old Testament saints, people coming to Christ in the Gospels before the start of the Church Age, and people coming to faith in the Lord Jesus after the pretribulation Rapture through the end of the Millennial Kingdom.

[2] Michael J. Vlach, *He Will Reign Forever* (Silverton, OR: Lampion Press, 2017), 218–219, 498–499.

[3] Alva J. McClain, *The Greatness of the Kingdom* (Winona Lake, IN: BMH Publishing, 1959), 434.

[4] McClain, 509.

[5] Mark Hitchcock, *The End: A Complete Overview of Bible Prophecy and the End of Days* (Carol Stream, IL: Tyndale House Publishers, 2012), 432.

[6] Randall Price, *The Temple and Bible Prophecy* (Eugene, OR: Harvest House Publishers, 1999), 531.

[7] Price, 556.

[8] Price, 554.

CHAPTER FIFTEEN

[1] "How much water is there on, in, and above the Earth?" The USGS Water Science School, December 2, 2016, water.usgs.gov/edu/earthhowmuch.html.

[2] Dr. S. Sanz Fernández de Córdoba, "100km Altitude Boundary for Astronautics," FAI Astronautic Records Commission, 2017, www.fai.org/page/icare-boundary.

[3] Flint Wild, ed., "What is an Orbit?" NASA Knows! (Grades 5-8), National Aeronautics and Space Administration, July 7, 2010, updated August 7, 2017, www.nasa.gov/audience/forstudents/5-8/features/nasa-knows/what-is-orbit-58.html.

[4] "Where is space?" The NOAA National Environmental Satellite, Data, and Information Service (NESDIS), February 22, 2016, www.nesdis.noaa.gov/content/where-space.

[5] "World Birth and Death Rates," Ecology Global Network, www.ecology.com/birth-death-rates.